A Rehabilitation of Say's Law

W. H. HUTT

A Rehabilitation
of Say's Law

OHIO UNIVERSITY PRESS: ATHENS

Preface

Since this essay was submitted to the publisher, a major work on an important aspect of the same subject has appeared: *Say's Law* by Tom Sowell.* This is a work of distinction. Its scholarly treatment of the controversies which Say's ideas provoked during the first half of the nineteenth century is, I judge, an important contribution to the history of economic thought. But Sowell's aim and mine are not quite the same. I shall be trying to rehabilitate the "law of markets" by showing "what Say really meant" or "what Say ought to have meant."

Moreover, Sowell may not accept all of my conclusions. He seems to me to be more neutral than I am on the main issue. In spite of his adverse criticisms being directed almost wholly at Say's detractors and occasionally against certain unsatisfactory arguments of Say's less rigorous disciples (such as McCulloch) Sowell is not led to claim that Say's law stands inviolate, which is the thesis that I am to advance. And on one crucial point I feel that he is definitely wrong. (*See* Chap. IV, pp. 35-36).

Although my own approach is very different, I am delighted that Sowell's erudite book has preceded mine. I warmly recommend it to the reader of my own contribution. I have been able to insert a few references to it at relevant points.

*T. Sowell, *Say's Law*, Oxford University Press, 1973.

At the galley proof stage, I became aware of yet another relevant contribution, which may turn out to be of pathbreaking importance. It is a recent article entitled "Say's Principle", by R. Clower and A. Leijonhufvud*. It is essential to draw attention to it. Previous works by these authors suggested that they were hesitant about the importance of Say's law. I discuss their earlier views at some length. But their treatment of "Say's principle" (which, as now explained, refers to a vital implication of Say's law rather than to the law itself) seems to me to record a significant development. The position of these economists is now much nearer to mine than appeared from their previous writings. The student is urged to read their latest treatment as corrective or supplementary to the argument I submit. Holding that "there is hardly a single problem in macro theory (or for that matter, micro theory) that can be consistently analyzed without . . . " a recognition of "Say's principle," they maintain that "the extensive literature since Keynes . . . has got bogged down in a mire of conceptual and semantic confusion." Their words here explain my incentive and why I devote the whole of Chapter II to definitions. I am trying to clear up the confusion.

I planned my contribution while I was a Visiting Research Fellow at the Hoover Institution, Stanford University, and Distinguished Visiting Professor of Economics at California State College, Hayward. I have actually written it while I have been Distinguished Visiting Professor of Economics at the University of Dallas, Irving, Texas.

---

*R. Clower and A. Leijonhufvud, *Say's Principle, What It Means and What It Does Not Mean* (*Intermountain Economic Review*, Vol. IV, No. 2, Fall, 1973).

Contents

	Preface	V
I	*Introduction*	1
II	*Definitions (with some Explanations)*	13
III	*Say's Law Restated*	24
IV	*Further Objections to Say's Law*	30
V	*The Concept of Withholding*	43
VI	*Unemployment Disequilibrium*	46
VII	*The True Multiplier*	53
VIII	*The Alleged Hiatus*	57
IX	*Yeager's Interpretation*	61
X	*"Effective Demand" in Relation to Saving Preference and Liquidity Preference*	66
XI	*The Hiatus—A Different Interpretation*	78
XII	*Pricing for Market Clearance*	89
XIII	*Sub-Optimal Employment and Chronic Unemployment*	103
XIV	*Harry G. Johnson's View of Pre-Keynesian Orthodoxy*	110

CONTENTS

XV *The Position of "the Prevailing Orthodoxy"
of the 1920s and 1930s* 116

XVI *Some Aspects of Edwin Cannan's "Orthodoxy"* 128

XVII *The Background of Keynes' "General Theory"* 134

XVIII *Conclusion* 145

I

INTRODUCTION

In his 1970 Richard Ely Lecture, Harry G. Johnson, without defending Keynesian doctrine, justifies Keynes' assault of 1936 (in *The General Theory*) on the prevailing economic orthodoxy, on the grounds that its "principles and slogans" (which, by implication, are apparently assumed to have activated policy before 1936) " . . . could neither explain nor cope with" the great depression.

While Keynes was writing his famous work I was engaged on a book that appeared a month or two later than his. In my contribution I maintained that "every independent and serious economist . . . must, if his beliefs lie in the path of 'orthodox' or Classical tradition, be aware of a periodic recurrence of a sense of utter helplessness. . . . He recognizes that in spheres in which policy and action can be influenced, he is doomed to virtual dumbness today."[1]* Thus, *where Johnson blames the prevailing orthodoxy of the 1930s,*

---

*I do not suggest that the "orthodox" economists could think of nothing to say! They felt frustrated by their perception that, owing to the absence of an understanding of the major issues among political leaders and electorates, their teachings would hardly have any chance of an influential hearing.

1

I blamed (in 1936) the ignoring of its basic teachings for the emergence and perpetuation of depression.

I can think of no economist who has shown greater intellectual courage than has Harry Johnson in abandoning previously held positions. Where he now stands in respect of the "law of markets," I do not know. But I believe that "the classical economists" who "from Smith to Pigou" (in Keynes' view and Mark Blaug's words) " . . . fell victims to Say's law"[2] were better economists because they *were* so victimized. I believe also that *with all their shortcomings* the non-Keynesians of the inter-war period had a deeper insight into the origins of chronic unemployment and depression than the overwhelming majority of today's professional economists. I shall try to substantiate this thesis after a restatement of Say's "law of markets" and an examination of typical criticisms of that law. At the end of my essay, in Chapters XIV to XVII, I shall briefly discuss the British situation in 1936 as well as "classical" teachings and government policies in Britain between the first world war and 1936. The environment of that period was one which somehow inspired the most influential book in the history of economic thought, the book which engendered the so-called "new economics" or the "Keynesian revolution" and, at a crucial period, destroyed the authority of the economists whom Johnson still disparages but towards whose position he seems (to me at any rate) to have been veering. I shall finally submit my own brief diagnosis of the grave sickness which was plaguing the British economy during the 1930s; and I shall suggest, (a) that exactly the same fundamental problem is baffling British politicians and opinion makers today that was baffling them in the 1920s and 1930s; and (b) that the solution is to be found through a perception of the light which Say's law throws upon the nature of co-operation in a free economy.

In defending the pre-Keynesian "classical economists," and "Say's law," I shall insist that this law dominated the prevailing orthodoxy of the 1930s so naturally that it was seldom if ever stated explicitly and (prior to the "Keynesian revolution") virtually never challenged. But it was ideas we associate with J. B. Say which constitute the vital insight of the "orthodoxy" that Keynes attacked. In one passage[3] Keynes explicitly recognized that the teachings he was trying to refute involved reliance on Say's law, although in that passage he referred not to Say himself but to J. S. Mill, from whom he quoted an excerpt out of a not very satisfactory exposition of the principle. (*See* p. 24).

I shall suggest that, fairly interpreted, "Say's law of markets" survives as the most fundamental "economic law" in all economic theory. It enunciates the principle that "demands in general" *are* "supplies in general" —different aspects of one phenomenon.

Today's textbooks usually express Say's law most carelessly, using a description of the law which, I think, Keynes was the first to use. It asserts, they tell their readers (without mentioning Keynes) that "supply creates its own demand".[*] But the supply of plums does not create the demand for plums. And the word "creates" is injudicious. What the law really asserts is that the supply of plums *constitutes* demand for whatever the supplier is destined to acquire in exchange for the plums under barter, or with the money proceeds in a money economy. (The supplier may of course hold on to the money, i.e., demand *it* instead of other non-money).

Controversy about the validity of this law (which occurred mainly in two periods—from 1803-1850 and from

[*] I believe that Keynes (*General Theory*, p. 18) was the first to use this phrase. It has been repeated *in these very words* by virtually all other economists who have since referred to Say's law. Even erudite and careful historians of economic thought repeat Keynes' words, e.g., Schumpeter, Mark Blaug and Tom Sowell, the latter opening his essay with Keynes' summary of the law and subsequently using the phrase several times.[4] But I cannot trace its ever having been used before Keynes. Sowell refers to it as a "familiar assertion," which he admits is not a "direct quotation" from Say or James Mill. Leijonhufvud uses it in quotation marks without attributing it to Keynes. (*On Keynesian Economics and the Economics of Keynes*, p. 280).

3

1936 until today) was described by the great Joseph Schumpeter as "a discussion which reflects little credit on all parties concerned." It has "dragged on to this day," he said, "with people armed with superior technique still chewing on the same old cud. . . . "[5] Well, more than two decades after the posthumous appearance of Schumpeter's monumental *History of Economic Analysis*, from which this scathing comment is quoted, I have been moved to keep the cud-chewing going. This is in spite of my agreement with Schumpeter (a) that Say did not *fully* understand the "law" to which his name has become attached[6]; and (b) that in his defence of the "law" against acute but economically illiterate critics, Say was sometimes very "woolly," slipping, at times, into serious fallacy.*

An occasional eccentricity of the erudite Schumpeter was reckless exaggeration. It was unjust of him to have written that Say "hardly understood his discovery himself." Certainly Say did not *fully* understand "the law of markets" which, I think, he regarded as accepted doctrine and not as *his* discovery. That is, I suggest, why James Mill did not refer to Say's chapter on markets in his *Commerce Defended* (a most impressive exposition of the "law"), while Say, in his second edition, did not mention James Mill's contribution which had appeared in between.* Both were explaining what they believed to be unchallengeable. Both attempted to convey to the business world, to governments and to students what the economists had learned from the Physiocrats, Hume and Adam Smith.

*Even so, Say's early phrasings of the "law of markets," some of which are quoted in Chapter III, are laudably clear and unequivocal: and his detractors during the earlier period can be not unfairly regarded as *"amateurs"* in economics, in comparison with those who, like Thornton, the Mills, Senior, Ricardo and McCulloch, were learned scholars in the subject. (Compare Sowell, *Say's Law*, pp. 220, 232).

*James Mill referred to Say as "a late French writer" and quoted an anecdote of Say's to illustrate the absurdity of regarding consumption as the source of demand.[7]

4

Schumpeter was by no means anti-Say, in spite of the harshness with which he treated him. Properly formulated, he said, Say's law is true, and "neither trivial nor unimportant."[8] But he thought that its main importance arose from its "negative" demonstration that general "restrictions of output" were no cure for crisis or depression. Such phenomena were "never to be causally explained solely by everybody's having produced too much."[9] This *is*, of course, a significant implication of the "law." But if the arguments I shall be developing in this book are valid, Schumpeter disclosed that, just like Say, he did not *fully* understand the "law of markets."

I propose to enunciate the proposition that the "law" has a much more positive meaning than Schumpeter perceived; that a grasp of it is indispensable for an understanding of the true genesis of depression and of prosperity without inflation; that attempts at dynamic treatment of the economic system which ignore it are worthless; that new "withholdings of inputs or outputs," mainly consequent upon the failure to price all such inputs and outputs for "market clearance" into consumption or stock accumulation, are the origin of depressed economies; that the path from that condition to non-inflationary prosperity is always *via* the dissolution of such "withholdings"; that this objective can be achieved only by institutional reforms aimed successfully at creating incentives for (and/or the removal of disincentives for) the pricing of all inputs and outputs for "market clearance"; and that such reforms facilitate the mechanism whereby (in the money economy) all inputs and outputs are (subject to inevitable human error) continually co-ordinated in the light of the current or expected value of the money unit.

As I understand it, and in my own words, the *source of demand* for any particular input or output produced is the flow of inputs and outputs of all the things which do not compete with it; for some part of that flow is destined to be exchanged for it.

"The source of demand" means "the power to demand." In other words, the power to demand any part of the flow of productive services springs from the flow of non-competing productive services.* Moreover, all producers of goods or services are always in a position to value or price their contribution so as to induce a demand from others for that portion of their inputs or outputs as they (the producers) do not demand (i.e., retain) for themselves, as investors or consumers (unless what they intended to be production turns out to be valueless and wasted—inadvertent consumption).

To most economists trained in the Keynesian or neo-Keynesian tradition, which today means the overwhelming majority of the younger economists in the United States and Britain, such a proposition may at first appear almost intuitively as preposterously wrong. They will feel that, in the actual world, where there is indirect exchange and the use of money, "effective demand" may be insufficient for reasons other than pricing. Only under hypothetical barter, they may protest, can Say's law hold. I have written this essay to refute such a view.

The basic notion of Say's law had been expressed several decades before Say's effective enunciation of it. For instance, the Physiocrats generally, as J. J. Spengler has pointed out, had recognized that "commerce consists, not in buying and selling, but in the exchange of goods and services for goods and services,"[10] and that *is* a very broad yet apt statement of "the law of markets." Josiah Tucker came near to stating the principle when he wrote, "the work of one man gives employment to another."[11] And Mercier de la Rivière,

---

*This statement holds without qualification in the absence of saving or dissaving. When saving is occurring, assets are being demanded through the offer of services (capital by the offer of income). When dissaving is occurring, services for consumption are being demanded through the offer of assets, *or* assets are themselves being consumed.

6

although accepting other ideas inconsistent with it, came even closer when he wrote, "no one can buy except by reason of what he sells."[12] But prior to Say, in spite of this recognition that *one purchases things with money's worth (and not with money, unless one's money holdings are being depleted)*, certain mercantilist, Keynes-like fallacies, largely contradictory with this insight, seem to have prevented any clear perception of the full implications. *

Turgot, however, discerned the confusion due to supposing that "saving and hoarding are synonymous," and insisted that although "savings" are made "in the form of money," the savers have no use for money "than to convert it *immediately* into different kinds of effects. . . . "[13] Turgot's statement is, of course, an exaggeration because it tacitly *assumes* that the prospective productivity of money is not changing in relation to that of non-money. But his tacit assumption is reasonable enough for most circumstances and his criticism of his contemporaries on the point had, I suggest, validity. It was because of the Physiocrats' misconceptions on the very issue Turgot had in mind that, in developing his "theory of markets," Say strongly criticized the school of economists from whom his inspiration may have originated. *

What Say was really showing was that the crucial nexus between *potential* sellers and *potential* buyers (*potential* suppliers and *potential* demanders) which,

---

*I am here thinking of such things as the confusion of saving-preference with liquidity-preference, the confusion of spending with demanding, the confusion of spending with consumption, the fear of general overproduction, the notion that consumption is the source of demands.

*I use the word "may" because I think that, apart from Turgot, Say's main inspiration came from Hume, Adam Smith and (possibly) James Mill, in whose works the confusion to which I have referred is absent. Of these, only James Mill stated the principle in general terms (in *Commerce Defended*, 1808), and his statement was better than Say's had been in the first edition of the latter's *Political Economy.*

7

when constrained, causes a slowing down of productive activity, is never constrained through the use of money or through monetary policy but *through defects in pricing.* Under the conditions of his day, no grounds existed for Say to add what it would have been appropriate to have added in the present era, namely, "even although deflation may magnify the consequences of defects in the pricing process and unanticipated inflation minimize those consequences" [my phrasing].

If Say's law holds, then any unemployment of *valuable* (i.e., potentially demanded) factors of production must be due to the supply of their services being *withheld.* And if supplies of non-competing productive services, which in the aggregate form *the source of* demands for *particular factors,* such as (say) for those used to make footwear, are being withheld, then the incentive may be enhanced to withhold also from production some part of the labor and assets which produce footwear. Such withholdings, *whether initiatory or induced,* may occur (i) through the direct holding off of potentially demanded supplies from the market, or (ii) (the same thing in practice) through *the price asked* being (a) higher than potential purchasers of the product *can afford* out of uninflated capital and income, or (b) higher than *they regard as profitable,* or (c) (a special case of [b]) higher than is consistent with *the cost and price expectations* of the community as a whole or with their predictions of the future of the market rate of interest.

In a situation in which widespread layoffs of men are occurring, and physical assets are being thrust into idleness, the withholding of supplies (directly or through pricing) *appears* as a sort of evaporation of demands, or as a sort of redundancy or excess of supplies, not as a *withholding* of supplies. Keynesian teaching accepts that appearance as reality. But I shall try to show that an understanding of Say's law exposes as basically fallacious the thesis, both in its Keynesian and its neo-

Keynesian enunciation, that the origin of depression is to be observed (a) in "excess" aggregate supply, or (b) in "deficient" aggregate demand, or (c) in aggregate demand somehow not being "effective."

Over the period 1940-1960, it was generally (but not universally) accepted that Keynes and his disciples had refuted Say's law through their establishment of the revolutionary "unemployment equilibrium" thesis. But for well over a decade now, through the friendly criticisms of eminent scholars like Haberler, McCord Wright, Modigliani and Patinkin, the "unemployment equilibrium" foundation of Keynes' thesis has ceased to be defended (although this quiet counter-revolution has not yet, I think, led to all the required textbook revisions).

Of more recent years Harry G. Johnson, R. W. Clower, Axel Leijonhufvud and Leland Yeager have continued the process of challenging the very foundations of the Keynesian system, in the process indirectly, if unintendedly, re-asserting Say's law. Yet paradoxically these eminent theorists, and other economists of repute who accept their criticisms of, or changing attitudes towards, the Keynesian system, still *seem* to leave the impression that, after all, Say's law does not work—at least not in the manner in which the old general equilibrium analysis suggested it did; and they suggest that in some way the world must feel grateful to Keynes, not so much for his contributions to economic method as for the beneficial policy consequences of his *General Theory* up to some unspecified turning-point some years ago.* There are healthy opinion differences among these economists; yet they all agree that there were *basic* defects in the economics that Keynes attacked, and their criticisms all *imply* dissatisfaction with Say's law. Their objections to the notion that supplies constitute

---

*E.g., R. W. Clower thinks that "however beneficial" the Keynesian revolution "may have been in *its practical effects* on a nearly decadent science, it added nothing novel or worthwhile to the *theoretical foundations* of economic science."[14]

the source of demands are always traceable, directly or indirectly (as I suggested before) to the surviving notion that *the use of money* somehow frustrates the operation of the market-clearing process. Under theoretical barter, the implication (or explicit assertion) is, Say's law *would* apply. In a money economy it does not.

One critic of a draft of this essay holds that Keynes regarded Say's law as a truism of no useful application. Certainly Keynes enunciated the law at one place— quite wrongly—as though it was an identity ("Walras' identity," *see* pp. 33-34). But early protagonists of the "Keynesian revolution" certainly did not take this line. They went to great trouble to refute Say; and I have felt it essential to devote Chap. IV and pp. 24-29, to evaluating some of their objections. Moreover, Keynes' "unemployment equilibrium" thesis, which the original Keynesian disciples proclaimed as *the* great insight of their leader, was obviously intended to be a refutation. In one of the most famous of the early defenses of *The General Theory*, Sweezy triumphantly admitted that "all" the arguments of that book "fall to the ground if the validity of Say's law is assumed."[15]

Although Say's law is no truism (indeed, I regard it as the most fundamental law in all economic theory) it is not difficult to grasp provided we are not confusing ourselves through defective notions. In my first reading of *The General Theory*, I was left with the impression that the crucial weakness of that book lay in its conceptual inadequacy. I developed this assertion in the *Theory of Idle Resources*, 1939,[16] and I made it clear that my main purpose was to establish conceptual clarity in respect of the notion of "unemployment" of men and assets. I devoted a special section to the general question of definitions in economics.* In the Preface of my *Keynesianism*, 1963, I referred to the feeling I acquired in verbal discussion with friends at the London School

---

*That section is one of the few parts of my 1939 book which I do not think I should amend today if I were thinking of republishing.

of Economics during 1949 and 1956, that I was "not talking the modern language." I explained how I had perceived "that *there are some kinds of language the habitual use of which hinders the perception of certain things as well as the saying of them*"; and how I had come to see "*that the weaknesses of the system which Keynes had built rest in its conceptual foundations*".[17] And my quarrel today with the surviving Keynesian influences which inspire attempts to inhibit recognition of Say's law is not with the manipulatory methods used but chiefly with the arbitrariness or sheer woolliness of the notions on which the critical models are constructed. In this essay therefore I shall at the outset carefully define certain very simple yet basic concepts as I shall be using them. This procedure alone may, I think, dissolve many predictable objections to my defense of the law of markets.

J. M. Keynes' *The General Theory of Employment, Interest and Money* (Macmillan, London, 1936) will be referred to throughout as *The General Theory*, and A. Leijonhufvud's *On Keynesian Economics and the Economics of Keynes* (New York, Oxford University Press, 1968) as *On Keynesian Economics*.

1. W. H. Hutt, *Economists and the Public* (London, Jonathan Cape, 1936), p. 34.

2. M. Blaug, *Economic Theory in Retrospect* (Homewood, Ill., Irwin, 1968), p. 154 n.

3. J. M. Keynes, *The General Theory* (See note above), p. 19.

4. T. Sowell, *Say's Law* (Princeton University Press, 1973), pp. 3, 4 (twice), 12, 19, 201.

5. J. A. Schumpeter, *History of Economic Analysis* (Oxford University Press, 1954), p. 625.

6. *Ibid.*, p. 625.

7. James Mill, *Commerce Defended* (London, C. and R. Baldwin, 1808), p. 76.

8. Schumpeter, *op. cit.*, p. 617.

9. *Ibid.*, p. 618.

10. J. J. Spengler, "The Physiocrats and Say's Law of Markets," in J. J. Spengler and W. R. Allen, *Essays in Economic Thought* (Chicago, McNally, 1960), p. 170.

11. Quoted in *Ibid.*, p. 204.

12. Quoted in *Ibid.*, p. 175.

13.   Quoted in *Ibid.*, pp. 205-6.
14.   R. W. Clower, *Monetary Theory* (London, Penguin, 1969), p. 20.
15.   P. Sweezy, "Keynes the Economist," in *Science and Society*, 1946, p. 300.
16.   W. H. Hutt, *Theory of Idle Resources* (London, Jonathan Cape, 1939).
17.   W. H. Hutt, *Keynesianism—Retrospect and Prospect* (Chicago, Regnery, 1963), p. ix.

II

DEFINITIONS (WITH SOME EXPLANATIONS)

Production. The creation of value (Say's definition). More rigorously, (a) *as a process,* provision of the flow of productive services by men or assets (natural resources being included under "assets"); and (b) *as a magnitude,* the "real" value of that flow.

This aggregate "real" value of the production flow —aggregate output, or aggregate real income, or whatever we call it— is not simply a question of the physical magnitudes of all the different outputs. It is a special measurement of the "creation of value," the measuring-rod being an abstractly conceived money unit of constant purchasing power, defined in an index number, the weighting of which is regarded as *appropriate* (although it cannot avoid being arbitrary).*

Consumption. The extermination of value (Say's definition). It is therefore the extermination of power to

---

*In my judgment such an index ought ideally, as far as is technically practicable, to give equal importance to every segment of the aggregate flow of productive services. But for many reasons, values of the flow of end products —which include the surviving values of previous services embodied into end products—must form the chief data for the construction of such an index.

demand. Both the creation and the extermination of value may occur passively.

Manna falling from heaven would have to be classed as "production" and the destruction of manna (say, by a flood) would have to be classed as "consumption". Consumption may be unintentional, purposeless or wasteful. A rise in the aggregate value of outputs is "production" and a decline in that value is "consumption." *

Supplies. Ignoring the case of barter, inputs or outputs (including accumulated outputs) offered at "money's worth" (*see* below), i.e., at prices which induce their sale to potential purchasers. That is, the magnitude of supplies in each case will depend upon the price asked, which will be the "money's worth."

Outputs of physically completed goods *of which (because the marketing services demanded by potential purchasers have not been fully provided) the full production process is incomplete* are also "supplied" to the owner (and "demanded" by him). They are not yet sold (purchased), but they are invested in as they replenish inventories or accumulate in the form of inventories. Just as materials may be "supplied" at their "money's worth" to replace or add to a potential purchaser's inventories, so will they be "supplied" without being sold (purchased), if they enter their *producer's* inventories (their *imputed value* being their "money's worth"). Entrepreneurs will *ceteris paribus* try to fix such prices as are calculated to maximize the "creation of value," that is the yield to investment in inventories.

"Production" is the source of "supplies"; but some portion of potential supplies may be "withheld" (by curtailment of production) for the advantage of potential suppliers. As the theory of monopoly demonstrates, a contrived scarcity of the flow of certain valuable things

---

*A rise in the value of outputs brought about by monopolistic restraint implies a reduction in the value of non-competing outputs.

(i.e., the "withholding" of potential supplies) may be to the advantage of those who own the flow; but while the "money's worth" of *that particular flow* may rise, the "money's worth" of *the aggregate flow* of output might decline under "monetary flexibility." (*See* p. 22.)

To supply. To offer inputs or outputs at prices or values which induce their sale, or investment in them, whether for replacement of consumption or the net accumulation of assets.

Demands. Offers for inputs or outputs which induce their providers to sell, or invest in them as prospectively profitable assets.

"Potential supplies" of and "potential demands" for things (at different values or prices) may be represented in supply schedules and demand schedules; but actual supplies and actual demands are identical magnitudes with identical values or prices at the point of intersection of those schedules.

Competing and non-competing inputs and outputs. Output A (say, margarine) is "competing" with output B (say, butter) if an increase in the flow of A, or a fall in its price, implies a fall in the *market-clearing price* of B, or a reduction in its supply. Similarly, output A is "non-competing" with output C (say, shoe polish) if an increased flow of A, or a fall in its price, has no discernible influence on the market-clearing price of C or tends either to raise that price or bring forth a greater supply. Of course, as Walras stressed, all outputs (whether of consumer's goods or of producer's goods) are competing for the demands of income receivers and owners of assets.

Competition. The substitution of a lower cost method of (a) producing and marketing any commodity or service or (b) of attaining any other objective (material or non-material, private or collective) which involves a cost (the sacrifice of any other commodity or valued objective), *irrespective of the institutional framework needed to create, release and/or protect incentives for the substitution.* Strictly speaking, the word "marketing" under (a) is redundant; for the various marketing processes are as important as all other ways of "creating value," such as farming, fishing, mining, transportation, manufacturing, and others.

Saving. The *process* of (a) replacing, partially or fully, the real value of that part of the stock of assets and the flow of services which is exterminated by consumption, in whatever sector of the economy the extermination occurs, or (b) adding to the stock of assets.

Savings. The net accumulation of value, i.e., the *magnitude* of the excess of value created (production) during a period over value exterminated (consumption) over that period.

Savers. To simplify exposition the term "savers" is used to mean "net savers," although "dissavers" (see below) who do not consume the whole value of their assets over a period, in replacing some part of the value they exterminate, are simultaneously performing the saving and dissaving processes. Savers so defined accumulate assets—capital—a prospective income-stream, by refraining from consuming a greater value than is created by their efforts and assets (their "production").

Dissavers. Those whose efforts and assets create insufficient value to offset the value they exterminate.

Saving preference. The aggregate expression of subjective valuations (preferences) as between consumption in the relatively distant future in contrast to consumption

16

in the relatively immediate future. As with all *changes* in preferences, the extent to which they evoke *actual supply responses* (at market-clearing prices) will depend upon the versatilities of men and assets, i.e., elasticities of supply under that condition. A positive response to a rise in saving preference is usually manifested as a growth in that proportion of *value created* (production) which is embodied into assets of long life, to value created by embodiment of services into assets of short life and/or the immediate extermination of value created when services are consumed as they are rendered.

Assets. "Stores of value" other than human beings who are not slaves. In a money economy, all things—tangible or intangible—which, through the prospective income-stream they provide, have "money's worth" are assets.

Investment. The entrepreneurial *process* of choosing the prospectively most profitable forms in which services are embodied into assets for replacement or accumulation, "human capital" (the composition of the stock of muscles and skills) included. That is, in this essay, *"investment" is not conceived* of as a magnitude. The relevant *magnitudes* are (i) "savings," or "net accumulation," and (ii) "dissavings" or "decumulation".

Money. All assets the value of which arises, or is enhanced, because they are demanded and held *wholly or partially* for the monetary services they render, i.e., for the express purpose of exchange for non-money goods or services in the future. This definition covers currency in circulation, demand deposits, *and* (here my usage differs from what is conventional°) the pure

---

°In the quantity theory identity $(MV \equiv PT)$ as I use it (purely for exposition purposes), M includes the pure money equivalent of "near money." As other economists use the identity the effects of "near money" are represented (most misleadingly in my judgment) under V.

17

money equivalent of "near-money" or "money substitutes"—"hybrid" assets which are partly non-money but which provide monetary services and are therefore partly money also ("hybrid assets").**

Income. The aggregate value of production—i.e., the flow of productive services rendered by men and assets. This flow includes those services (a very small proportion) which are finally consumed as they are rendered, and those embodied into assets (short-life inventories or long-life "fixed assets") which replace (wholly or partially) the value of consumption or contribute to the net accumulation of assets. *Income* may be measured in actual money units, such as dollars or pounds ("money income") or in abstractly conceived units of defined constant purchasing power ("real income").

Income may be broken down into the yield to labor and the yield to the owners of assets. Either of these yields may be contractual or residual, according to whether owners or workers accept responsibility for the success of productive operations and hence bear the risk. When the yields are contractual, they are known as "wages" and "interest" respectively. In the present essay it will be assumed for simplicity (and not unrealistically) that the yield to labor is wholly *contractual*, the entrepreneurial function being undertaken solely on behalf of the owners of assets,* with the yield being, therefore, residual—that is, interest *plus* profits or *minus* losses.

Money income. The aggregate value of the flow of productive services, measured in actual money units

** On the notion of the "pure money equivalent" of such "hybrid" assets, see Hutt, *Keynesianism*, p. 92.

* This assumption is relaxed on p. 106, first footnote.

(e.g., dollars), whether directly consumed or embodied into assets. Money income contributes to aggregate "money-spending power" (as distinct from "purchasing power"). But assets are "stores of value" and hence also contribute to "money-spending power" at their "money's worth."

Money's worth. That price at which any chosen quantity of a thing (be it services or assets) can be sold *at any moment.* Any chosen portion of the stock of assets, or of the flow of inputs, or of the flow of outputs is always realizable immediately for money, without cost, at its "money's worth," even if, through entrepreneurial misjudgement, this worth is influenced (i) by the services or assets having been produced in unprofitable abundance or (ii) by decisions to liquidate inventories more rapidly than is destined to maximize the yield from investment in them. In the extreme case, the "money's worth" of *outputs* could be nil, in which event consumption equal to the value of the inputs will have occurred. "Money's worth" may be determined under social discipline, i.e., under "free" competitive market pressures, or in the private interest (as *via* governmental "controls," or private coercion, or collusion)°

Market-clearing price. A particular case of "money's worth"; namely, that price at which such portion of the flow of services or of the stock of assets as the pro-

---

°The implication that "all goods are perfectly liquid" (Leijonhufvud's phrase) at their "money's worth" does not require the condition of "general competitive equilibrium". Nor does it mean that "the full value of any good can be instantly realized", as Leijonhufvud suggests (*On Keynesian Economics*, p. 79), if the term "full value" means "market-clearing value". But if the ambiguous term means "money's worth", the implication of perfect liquidity (instant realization) *does* exist.

vider or owner does not judge it profitable to invest in or judges it profitable to disinvest from, can be sold at any moment *in the absence of any "withholding of capacity" on his part. In the case of inputs,* market-clearing prices ("costs") are those which induce investment in all inputs which lack more remunerative fields of utilization, because prospective yields to the entrepreneurial intermediary from all increments acquired exceed or do not fall short of the market rate of interest.

Withheld capacity. Labor and assets that are idle or idling through a defect in the pricing system, i.e., through a failure to price their services for "market clearance." Such a defect can occur (i) because prices are fixed (by law, through private duress, or through collusion) in the private interests of the suppliers or demanders of the services priced; or (ii) (simply a special form of "exploitative" pricing) because men or assets have, through various devices and stratagems, including discernible private duress, been shut out from particular areas, occupations or firms.

The distinction between (a) the "withholding" of outputs through the charging of values or prices above market-clearing values, and (b) the productive accumulation of outputs in the form of inventories or additions to physical plant and equipment is to be dealt with in several contexts. My *Theory of Idle Resources,* 1939, tried to explain this issue through a distinction between *"pseudo*-idleness" and wasteful idleness (in assets and men). An entrepreneur may have to invest in materials at prices raised by cartel action and invest in labor at wage-rates forced up by strike-threat duress. Such materials and labor will have a "money's worth" which exceeds "market-clearing" values. But the entrepreneur himself may possess no similar power to contrive scarcities, and the price he must ask to clear the outputs which he judges will maximize his yield (given labor and material prices *above* the "market-clearing" level) will then be *"market-clearing"* under our definition.*

Monetary services. The contribution of money to production and hence to income; in other words, the *value created* by money held either (i) in households [mainly case (a), below] or (ii) in the course of production for exchange or sale. Monetary services are either (a) consumed as they are rendered, in which case money must be envisaged as a form of consumer assets creating value in the form of immediately consumed "gratifications"—security, convenience, etc.; or (b) embodied, as inputs, into the stock of assets [of short or long life], in which case money must be envisaged as a form of producer assets.

The money supply. The aggregate value of money measured in actual money units, such as dollars, pounds, francs, yen, or marks. It is often called "the nominal quantity of money." In my book *Keynesianism* I called it at times "the number of money units," to stress the reality that each unit can be envisaged as *a container* of "purchasing power," and that the magnitude of the contents of the containers can vary.

In the case of money and monetary services, "market-clearing *values*"* are prices of non-money which induce persons or corporations (for reasons of relative prospective profitability of money and non-money) either (a) *to supply money*, by decisions not to replenish their investments in money inventories as they are depleted through purchases, or (b) *to demand money* by accumulating money received, thereby increasing their investment in it.

°This point is further considered in Chapter V.

°To talk of the "price of *money*" is a slovenly use of language. Price is the valuation of non-money in terms of money. Today's tendency to refer to *the rate of interest* as the "price of money" is worse than slovenly. The metaphor indicates a serious confusion of thought.

Monetary flexibility. A monetary policy in which the treasury and/or the central bank (or other monetary authority) is under an obligation so to adjust or control the issue and withdrawal of *credit* (mainly deposits, notes, token money, and the pure money equivalent of "hybrid money" (*see* pp. 18-19) that, as far as is practicable, "the money supply" shall vary in direct proportion to the aggregate *real* value of money (i.e., "the money supply" measured in abstractly conceived money units of constant purchasing power). In other words, a monetary policy is *flexible* when the "money supply" can expand or contract sensitively, so as to be neither inflationary nor deflationary; and that means, in practice, when (through budgetary deficits or surpluses, open market operations, rediscount action, reserve ratio discipline and control of the note issue) the market rate of interest is maintained at what is judged to be the non-inflationary, non-deflationary level. * Under monetary flexibility, an appropriate price index will oscillate within a narrow amplitude about a constant trend of zero. The money unit can then be said to be "convertible in real terms."

Monetary rigidity. A condition in which "the money supply" fails to respond sensitively in either direction when the demand for money varies. In other words, monetary policy is rigid when "the money supply" remains unchanged, or does not vary in direct proportion to changes in the demand for money, so that the real value of the money unit (the "purchasing power" in each "container") may rise or fall.

Loss-avoidance, profit-seeking incentives. Incentives for responsible entrepreneurial action, that is, incentives to compete. Such incentives can be created, released or protected through institutions designed to prevent *as far as practicable* "the contrivance of scarcities" or "the

---

* I.e., at the Wicksellian "natural level."

22

contrivance of plenitudes,"* i.e., to prevent monopolistic or monopsonistic abuse (including oligopolistic or oligopsonistic abuse).

Exploitation. Any action taken, whether or not through discernible private coercion (collusion) or governmental coercion, or whether through monopolistic or monopsonistic power, which, under a given availability of resources (including the stock of knowledge and skills), reduces the value of the property or income of another person or group of persons, or prevents that value from rising as rapidly as it otherwise would, *unless this effect is brought about through* (a) the dissolution of some monopolistic or monopsonistic privilege, or (b) the substitution of some cheaper method (labor-saving or capital-saving) of achieving any objective (including the production and marketing of any output); or (c) the expression of a change in consumers' preference; or (d) through taxation authorized by explicit legislation accepted as legitimate in any context.

*I have explained the meaning of these terms elsewhere. See W. H. Hutt, *The Strike-Threat System*, Chapter VII; "Natural and Contrived Scarcities," *South African Journal of Economics*, 1935.

III

SAY'S LAW RESTATED

I propose now to attempt a re-exposition of Say's law, as I understand it, and then to deal briefly and broadly with the principal objections which were advanced against it prior to 1960. Following that, I shall discuss some more recent and more subtle arguments which may *appear* to question its validity or relevance.

Keynes' own reference to the law was based upon a quotation, not from Say's own enunciation, but from a rather unsatisfactory exposition of the idea in J. S. Mill's *Principles of Political Economy*; and the passage Keynes quoted was torn from a context which throws essential light upon its implications.* The young economists at Cambridge whose outlook Keynes found congenial and with whom he discussed his developing ideas, must surely have been unaware of Mill's incomparably more satisfactory treatment of the same topic in his *Unsettled Questions in Political Economy* (pp. 69-73), or they could hardly have failed to draw his attention to it.* I

*See W. H. Hutt, *Keynesianism*, p. 389-391.

*At least three other economists (Emil Korner, B. M. Anderson, Patinkin) have drawn attention to Keynes' surprising omission of the qualifying passage which followed, a passage which drew attention to some of the very issues he was ignoring.

feel even more certain that they could not have been aware of James Mill's astonishing *Commerce Defended* (1808) which is a better exposition of Say's law than Say's original enunciation of it. My own judgment is that neither Keynes himself, nor those of his colleagues who influenced him, had really grasped the "law of markets" to which Say's name has become attached. Let us consider what Say himself wrote.* "One can only buy with what one has produced,"[1] i.e., out of one's savings or income. "The one product constitutes the means of purchasing another."[2] Here Say was quietly asserting that one buys with money's worth, not with money, one's stocks of which are normally subject merely to temporary depletion. He used the term "value" for what I have called "money's worth," and described it as "the sole substance with which one buys".[3] "A product created offers, *from that instant*, a market for other commodities to the full total of its value"[4] [Say's italics]. Particular commodities "exceed the aggregate need people have for them, either because they have been produced in undue quantities, or rather because other outputs are deficient. Some commodities are superabundant because the production of other commodities has come to be in short supply (*sont venus à manquer*)."[5] "When the clearance of their products is slow . . . ," entrepreneurs say that "money is scarce."[6] A merchant will say, "*It is not other products that I am demanding in exchange for mine, it is money.*"[7] [Say's italics]. The answer to him is, "Sales are sluggish (*la vente ne va pas*), not because money is scarce but because other products are."[8]* I have won-

---

*The first two quotations are from the first edition of Say's *Political Economy* (*Traité d'Economie Politique*), 1803. The remainder are from the fourth edition, 1819. [The translations are mine.]

*James Mill's statement of the principle in 1808 is worth quoting. "The production of commodities . . . is the one and universal cause which creates a market for the commodities produced." "The collective means of payment of the whole nation . . . consist in its annual produce." "A nation's power of purchasing is exactly measured by its annual produce."[9] "The one part of (the annual produce) is employed in purchasing the other."[10]

dered at times how Keynes could have continued with *The General Theory* if he had quoted passages like these for refutation instead of that unsatisfactory passage from J. S. Mill.

I remarked at the outset that Say's law implies that all outputs constitute *"power* to demand," in the sense of *"power* to supply by valuing inputs and outputs at money's worth." Now it may be objected that *"power* to demand" in this sense does not mean *"willingness* to demand." I can refrain from selling (or exchanging for other assets or outputs) any part of the output produced by my labor or produced through the services of the assets I own. But in that case I am myself demanding what I produce. The fact that I do not *pay money* for it is irrelevant. A farmer is demanding that part of his produce which is destined to be consumed by himself or his family. And in a money economy the output he does not sell has a money value. If he consumes, say, one *per cent* of the potatoes he produces, that consumed part of his supply is demanded by him and must be valued at the market price realized by the 99 *per cent.* Hence *all exercised "power to supply" is exercised "power to demand." There are no imaginable exceptions.* *

This assertion will, I know, still prompt immediate and vehement objections. I shall be told that power to produce (and hence power to supply) *is* a question of will and the power may not be exercised. *That is cer-*

---

*To the extent to which I prefer leisure to the output of my labor (or to what I can realize from that output) I am demanding and consuming an immaterial but valuable thing—"valuable" because I must make a sacrifice of alternatives of money value in order to acquire it (just as I must *buy* an immaterial thing of money value when I purchase a house on a particularly beautiful or convenient site). Nevertheless, an increased demand for leisure by an individual *does* mean a reduced contribution from him to the source of demands as a whole, to the extent to which his supply of valuable output to others (priced to "clear the market") is reduced. From the standpoint of the economy as a whole every increase in the consumption of leisure has the same depressive effects as all other forms of consumption that are not accompanied by replacement equal to the value exterminated.

tainly possible, but it is an assertion of, not an objection to, Say's law. All power to demand is derived from production and supply. Because the extermination of value through consumption of services and assets is continuous, *the failure to supply* (i.e., the failure to produce, and price to induce the sale of sufficient goods and services to cover the full replacement of the value consumed) means the extermination of some part of the previous power to demand. Indeed, "consumption" in itself *is* the extermination of the power to demand, although *the need or wish to consume motivates the will to produce, via reliance on the need or wish to replace.* The process of supplying—i.e., the production and appropriate pricing of services or assets for replacement or growth—keeps the flow of demands flowing steadily or expanding. Hence, there *is* a meaning which can be attached to the phrase "willingness to demand". It simply means "willingness to supply"! (I return to this point in Chapter V.)

I expect also the objection that I am ignoring the possibility of monopsonistic abuse, which by definition means the withholding of some part of the full power to demand—a failure to demand all that could be demanded; and that monopsonists who exploit* in this manner are not (in that role) withholding "supplies"—the inputs and outputs *their* efforts and assets provide: they are simply curtailing their demands.

The answer is that they are *supplying* (in return for whatever they buy in the monopsonized field) a smaller "real value", i.e., a smaller *quantum* of whatever goods and services those from whom they buy are destined to acquire with the money received. Such effects, which are depressive on the economy, *illustrate* Say's law. Except for the case in which the suppliers are themselves the demanders, Say's law directs attention to actual *transactions*—the values

---

*See definition of "exploitation," p. 23.

(prices) of services and assets which are necessarily demanded when they are actually supplied. The adverse effects of monopsonistic abuse, if and when it occurs,* will be to reduce *profitable* supplies—inputs and outputs—in the field from which the monopsonists purchase, even if competition is effective among the suppliers so that there is no "withholding" on the latter's part. When, however, the monopsonists are frustrated (partially or wholly) by rigidly priced supplies, or by retaliatory monopolistic action, the deleterious repercussions are *likely* to be aggravated (although theoretically amelioration is possible). It is through those *contractions of supplies* which have their origin in "exploitation," however caused, that a general running down of the economy may be set in motion—through cumulative withholdings caused by rigidities *elsewhere in the pricing system.*

Hence whether a price for any commodity is imposed above the competitive equilibrium level by monopolistic power, or imposed below that level by monopsonistic power, the supply of the commodity—the amount that will be *actually* supplied and so *actually* demanded —will contract (unless extremely unrealistic assumptions are made. (See p. 48 and p. 81). That is, *the depressive effects upon the economy are similar irrespective of whether the initiating distortion of the pricing system is due to monopolistic or monopsonistic abuse.* In both cases, a reduction in supplies is caused, which, through a sort of chain reaction in the form of induced reductions in supplies of noncompeting outputs, creates an impression of a drying-up of demands.

The most serious attempt at refutation of Say's law in *The General Theory* is to be found in the unemployment equilibrium thesis, which I have examined elsewhere,[12] and which has been riddled with devasting

---

*Actually, for reasons I have explained elsewhere, I believe monopsonistic abuse to be of little *practical* importance.[11]

criticism—without effective rejoinder—by several economists of eminence.* In the following chapter I shall examine certain *other* objections which have been advanced against Say's law.

*See p. 9.

1. J. B. Say, *Political Economy*, 1st Edition. Quoted from J. J. Spengler in "The Physiocrats and Say's Law of Markets," in *Essays in Economic Thought*, Eds. Spengler and Allen, p. 213.
2. *Ibid.*
3. Say, *Political Economy*, 4th Edition, Book I, p. 153.
4. *Ibid.*, p. 153.
5. *Ibid.*, p. 154.
6. *Ibid.*, p. 148.
7. *Ibid.*, p. 149.
8. *Ibid.*, p. 151.
9. James Mill, *Commerce Defended*, p. 81.
10. *Ibid.*, p. 84.
11. W. H. Hutt, *The Strike-Threat System*, Arlington House, 1973, Ch. VIII.
12. W. H. Hutt, *Keynesianism*, Ch. IX.

IV

FURTHER OBJECTIONS
TO SAY'S LAW

A common objection alleges that the "law of markets" tacitly assumes away changes in the demand for money and, in particular, overlooks those variations in that demand which are not correlated with real output. It is the latter charge which is most serious. There certainly are reasons why, aggregate real income being given, people's preferences for the services of money, or their valuation of the productivity of money held may alter—seasonally, temporarily or permanently—including changes in custom, or habit, or business procedures. And there are certainly reasons for speculative variations: forecast changes in particular costs or prices; or forecast changes in the general price index; or forecast changes in the rate of interest.* But none of these sources of variations in demand for monetary services, of which every monetary policy must take cognizance, affects the relevance of Say's law. Yet economists of deserved eminence—not only

---

*Nearly all modern economists would include also the *absolute* level of the rate of interest as a factor influencing the demand for money. Although I am awed by the weight of authority against me on this issue, I have never been able to accept this.

the Keynesians—have read into the law, with no justification whatsoever, *an assumption* that the law implies "a marginal propensity to spend out of income equal to unity," or that "transactors never plan to change the amount of money they hold," or that the demand for money and the "money supply" vary in direct proportion to one another. The maintenance of this last relationship (i.e., what I have termed "monetary flexibility") is wholly a matter of "monetary policy." But it is to be part of my case that the issues involved in "monetary policy," are comprehensible only if the relevance of those issues to Say's law are perceived.

Say showed why, under the institutional setup of the era in which he was writing, the supply of money increased as the growth of trade led to an increased demand for the services of money,* but he did not rely upon this very important source of monetary flexibility to justify his "law of markets." Nor is that law invalidated (as Neisser contends[2]) because deflations (purposeful or inadvertent) can occur and, under downward price rigidity, result in depression and unemployment. On the contrary, the cumulative depressive effects of price rigidity in deflation (or in curbed inflation) *are explained by it.* Supplies (and hence demands) are *withheld* cumulatively, a point to which we must return.

We can perceive the relevance of money in relation to Say's law only when we recognize that the law is concerned with the nature of the supplying and the demanding of *all* valuable services and assets, money and the services of money ("liquidity") included. Investment in or disinvestment from inventories of money has no special significance. We invest in (or disinvest from) money —whether we want it as a producers' good or as a consumers' capital good—up to the point at which further

*A passage in Say's exposition in which this is clear is, curiously enough, quoted in one of the best known attacks on Say's law, that by Neisser.[1]

*On the *concept* of "withholding", *see* pp. 20-21 and Chapter V.

31

increments promise a yield below prospective yields from any form of non-money. A perception that all increments of money possessed have been acquired in the expectation that they will yield income, just as with inventories of non-money (fixed or circulating assets), assists perception of the all-pervasiveness of Say's law. People's forecasts of the yields to money (in the light of current judgments of monetary policy) give rise to what we call "demand for money."*

J. S. Mill, in one of his less rigorous moods, referred to what he thought was a significant fact, namely, that a seller need "not buy at the same time when he sells." Of course a seller may invest in money when he is paid! Mill was clearly envisaging the case in which the individual—and, by implication, the community—happen temporarily to choose (from preference or entrepreneurial judgment) relatively more monetary services or money, and hence to choose relatively less of non-monetary services or non-money assets (at their initial prices). Whether or not the bidding up of the aggregate real value of money, which such a change of choice implies, means a bidding up also of the real value of the *money unit* (as it must, under monetary rigidity), it is difficult to see in what sense "both commodities and money may then be in excess supply," as one Keynesian put it a few years ago. If the rise in the aggregate real value of money is due to expectations that monetary policy intends to raise the real value of the *money unit* and the expectations are correct, then speculative demands for money will assist the monetary aim. If the expectations are wrong, the speculators will be penalized. But in any case, I do not see how Say's law will be affected.

Similarly, to take the opposite case, when the relative value of investment in inventories of *non-money* assets

---

*Erroneous entrepreneurial predictions may of course bring about excess holdings of money or anything else. The productiveness of money is discussed fully in W. H. Hutt, "The Yield to Money Held," in *Freedom and Free Enterprise*, Ed. Sennholz, Van Nostrand, 1956.

increases because people expect their money value to rise, no one would say that there is an "excess" of such goods. The capital embodied in them is productively employed in the creation of prospective "time utilities." The only circumstances in which the word "excess" is really appropriate in this context is when it refers to the type of disequilibrium in which inventories are generally accumulating because (owing to entrepreneurial misjudgment or some non-market dictate) they are not being disposed of at prices sufficiently low to maximize the yield from the distribution of their sale over time. This is the "classical" notion of "excess." And the *prices* asked for such goods, rather than their "supplies" (as rates of output or as inventories) are then "excessive." It is of course common today to describe "disequilibrium" in respect of any particular input or output as "excess supply" or "excess demand." But under either situation, as Walras perceived, the prices and quantities of *actual* supplies (what he called "effective supplies") are equal to the prices and quantities of *actual* demands ("effective demands"). (*See* "Demands", p. 15). Recognition of this truism does not prevent a perception that erroneous forecasting may lead to oversupplies of particular outputs with consequential undersupplies of other outputs.

Marx's truism, "no one can sell unless someone else purchases," which some Keynesians believe illustrates a vital defect in Say's law, can be answered with the converse: "no one can purchase unless someone else sells." For every act of selling and buying requires that the *would-be seller* price his product to permit the sale or that the *would-be buyer* offer a price which the seller accepts. *Is not this price determination the root co-ordinative act which keeps a money economy in activity?*

Keynes thought that Say's law asserted that the "aggregate demand price of output is equal to its aggregate supply price for all volumes of output."[3] But this is not Say's law: it is "Walras' identity," which is a sophisticated statement of the obvious.* Because the price of every sale equals the price of the purchase, aggregate sales must always equal aggregate purchases. Each transaction can be looked at from two angles!

The recognition of such a tautology brings out, indeed, the irrelevance of money to Say's law. No matter how the purchasing power of the money unit may happen to be changing, the aggregate money value of sales and purchases (and hence the aggregate money value of such supplies and demands as are expressed through the use of money) must be identical. When I sell fruit grown in my garden, what I receive and what the purchaser pays me are the same! *But what is equally true, and what illustrates Say's law, is that I dispose of an identical value out of the money's worth I receive from that sale* whatever I am destined to acquire in return for it; and what I acquire will be of identical value. This remains true (a) whether I invest in additional money, by simply retaining an additional money balance equal to the value of the fruit I sell, or (b) whether my consumption of goods and services increases by the value of my proceeds from the sale (or by something less than that), or (c) whether I invest t'.e value of my sale in the replacement of goods and services being currently consumed, or (d) whether I do more than maintain the value of my assets intact and invest in additional non-money assets.

Another disparagement of Say's law attributes to it a tacit assumption that products must always realize prices corresponding to the expectations of those who have invested in their production. But there is no implication that every increment of an output or every output as a whole must always yield a value in excess of what the value of its inputs had been (interest being regarded as part of the value of inputs). Yet two of the most influential attacks on the law, those of Lange and Neisser,[5] have alleged that this is a necessary implication. A

*Modern economists *call* it "Walras' identity." But Quesnay stated the truism, "every purchase is sale, and . . . every sale is purchase".[4]

thing which is worth less than it cost may still have a positive value, which means that there is a potential demand for it; and the fact that such things *may* exist, and normally they *do* exist, does not weaken the vital law for which Say has been given credit. It does not detract from the reality that, in the absence of net capital consumption, the sole source of demand for any valuable output is the flow of non-competing outputs. When costs have not been covered, a smaller aggregate real value has been contributed to the flow of outputs (the source of demands) than would have resulted under ideal resource allocation, that is all. What Say's law does imply relevant to the issue is that products, however unprofitably or wastefully manufactured, need never themselves be *wasted*. If the output is *valueless*, it is not a product! *Consumption* will have occurred when resources were devoted to its manufacture—wasteful consumption. But all products (including services) can always be priced or valued for market clearance, i.e., to permit their consumption (or use in subsequent stages of production, or incorporation into other products), no matter how unprofitable their production may have been.

Sowell maintains that we can conceive of circumstances in which, because the value of aggregate output is less than its cost of production or its supply price, "*there can be a general glut*,"[6] and he italicizes those words. But as we have seen (*assuming monetary flexibility* as I have defined it) when so many outputs yield less than the rate of interest on the marginal increment invested in their respective inputs that *the money value of the sum of all outputs falls short of the sum of what sales of inputs as a whole had been*, there must have been *inadvertent net consumption*. Any such net extermination of value—unplanned dissavings—means that the source of future demands will have contracted. If that condition is to be described as "glut," then *we are conceiving of it as the consequence of over-consumption,*

not of under-consumption; and that is the diametric
opposite of what Say's critics have imagined.

Exactly the same considerations apply when "the aggregate value of output is less than . . . its supply
price." In Sowell's sense, the "supply price" of any
output means (in my terminology) the sum of the input
values incorporated in it (including marketing services
and interest *plus* profit or *minus* loss); and under
the relationship stipulated, the implication is that inputs
in general are priced above their market-clearing value.
Some portions of the potential contributions to the
"supplies" and hence to the source of demands are being
withheld.

There is nothing in either situation imagined to prevent
market-clearing prices from being re-established from
that point on, whether the reason for the contraction in
the source of demands has been (a) the over-pricing of
inputs through the seeking of private or sectional gains
via what I have termed the "withholding" process, or
(b) widespread entrepreneurial errors (of prediction or
otherwise) which adversely affect the composition of
the stock of assets. Neither "unemployment equilibrium"
nor "unemployment disequilibrium" is implied.

It seems sometimes to be suggested that Say's law
assumes that a changing scale of prices (rising or falling
prices in general) must be neutral in its effects upon
prices at different stages of production. But as we shall
see, economists who would never have thought of challenging that law knew perfectly well that unanticipated
inflation could have co-ordinative ("stimulative") effects
under conditions of cost rigidity. But in so far as the
raising of prospective final prices relatively to prospective costs brings about recovery (through the community not realizing what is occurring), Say's law *explains*
why this happens. The release of withheld capacity in
one industry contributes to the source of demands for
products in non-competing industries and tends therefore
to induce the release of capacity in them also.

A tenaciously held view is that Say's law dogmatically assumes away the reality of "underconsumption." But variations in saving-preference (i.e., in the propensity to consume) are irrelevant to the law. Changes in *all* preferences, unless responded to by changes in resource allocation (and that necessarily means changes in *relative* prices), result in the disco-ordination of the economy —a less fruitful utilization of productive capacity, including the emergence of wasteful and sometimes chronic idleness. When saving-preference (the propensity to save) rises, demands for directly consumed services or for productive services being embodied into goods of relatively short life (consumers' goods) will fall in relation to demands for productive services being embodied into goods of relatively long life (producers' goods). In addition the value of assets of long life will tend to be bid up in relation to inventories of goods of short life. A fall in saving-preference (a rise in the propensity to consume) will have the opposite effect. But both give rise to the same sort of adjustment problems. A *general decline* in the desire to provide for the future can create as many difficulties in pricing for market clearance as *a general rise* in that desire.

In my judgment, failures to adjust prices to changes in saving-preference have been of little importance as a causal factor in the phenomena of boom and depression. If this judgment is wrong, however, it does not invalidate my claim that Say's law explains any running down of activity in the situation imagined. It occurs when there are new failures to price for market clearance. All the cumulative depressive effects experienced during emerging recession have their origin in a succession of withholdings of supplies which an initial failure to co-ordinate to a change in preference or supply has brought in its train. *Depression is, indeed, the consequence of cumulatively-induced refusals to sell at prices consistent with the co-ordination of the economy.* This is the truth which Say's law ruthlessly exposes. Disco-ordination in

37

one sector of the economy will, if there are price rigidities in other sectors, bring about these successively aggravating reactions, one decline in the flow of services inducing another.

The fallacious notion of *general* under-consumption is related of course to the equally fallacious notion of *general* over-production. There is, in fact, no inconsistency (as some Keynesians have alleged) in Say's admission of the possibility of *particular* over-production or glut, while he denied the possibility of *general* over-production or glut. There *can* be "too much" of any commodity, but only in the sense that there is too little of another. Say could not have been more explicit on this point. Yet Keynesian and neo-Keynesian theories of over-production maintain that the *whole flow of productive services can be too big* in some sense. Say's law suggests that notions of "excess over-all productive capacity" or of "excess aggregate supply" are meaningless because demands consist simply of the offer of one part of this flow for other parts. Each demand expressed and effected is a supply offered and accepted. Hence the failure to demand the full flow of valuable services (and I must repeat that services *are* always valuable or they are not to be classified as services, while being valuable *means* they are capable of being demanded) must be due to the pricing (or valuing) of part of the flow too high in relation to the rest of the flow.

If this is understood, it should be obvious that "over-all productive capacity" can no more be "in excess" than can "over-all purchasing power." For the release of withheld (unutilized) productive capacity, through the pricing for market clearance of previously over-priced productive services (i.e., through the pricing of inputs and outputs consistently with the money valuation of income and price expectations) is, in itself, *the release of withheld purchasing power* (as distinct from money-spending power). In recession, a restoration of aggregate *purchasing power* need not be sought through an increase of *money-spending power*; although, under monetary flexibility, the flow of purchasing power and the flow of money-spending power will be correlated (through policy).

Chronic idleness of productive capacity in general is not due to its being "in excess." Say's law explains how a widespread laying-off of men, together with idleness or idling in the complementary assets with which they work, is temporarily inevitable as long as chronic disco-ordinations in the pricing system are tolerated; and if the disco-ordinations (price-cost ratios incompatible with full market clearance) are not rectified, the idleness will persist until the unutilized assets or the unemployed people find sub-optimal employments.* For instance, if unions persuade their members to resist such downward wage-rate adjustments as are needed to increase their own numbers in employment, as well as to contribute to a rise in the wages-flow and the income-flow, they are transforming temporary idleness into long-term idleness or (under certain conditions) chronic idleness.

Say's law does *not*, then, "assume full employment" or imply that full employment is achievable whatever pricing (valuing) policies are adopted. It does *not* imply that market pressures will always be allowed to bring about pricing for market-clearance. What it *does* imply is that market pressures *could*, if permitted, have this effect. It certainly does not assume, for instance, that the workers generally *will* behave in their own interest in such situations. In showing that the pricing of inputs and outputs for recovery and prosperity is *possible*, it relies on no assumptions at all about whether the co-ordination demanded is either practically achievable or politically conceivable. But it does explain why, no matter what monetary policy happens to be, inappropriate pricing can withhold supplies (thereby withholding demands), forcing valuable resources into temporary idleness or

*See pp. 55-56, 103-108

into less profitable activities, or causing loss of value; and *inter alia* how "inflationary recession" ("stag-flation") is possible.

If over-pricing is ruled out, then although *misdirected* production can occur (in the sense of particular over-productions which may cause some increments of assets replaced or accumulated—including inventories of final products—to be less profitable than had been pre-dicted, or saleable only at less than they had cost, or even to be valueless), this is a defect in the *composition* of aggregate output, not evidence of its *oversupply.* Defects in the composition of real income *reduce* its "quantity"—its value magnitude in money units of un-changing "purchasing power."

Some have thought that Say's law is valid only as a long-term theorem; that it would hold under "perfect price flexibility"; but that it is irrelevant to the price-rigid world of reality. It depends, so it is believed, upon the assumption that, although demands may be insuffi-cient to clear markets at any moment, they may be relied upon to do so ultimately. Actually, the law simply makes clear that, in so far as inputs or outputs *are* actually supplied, by being priced for sale, they are *at that moment*—with no time lag—demanding non-competing things.* This perception of the universal relevance of the law does not prevent recognition of the fact that pressures tending to bring about the pricing needed for market clearance cannot be expected to work instantaneously, especially after long periods in which policy has been designed to reduce or restrain the required pressures. But such sluggishness in the pricing process (as with all other inertias and "imperfections" in the operation

---

*(*See* definitions, pp. 19-20) "Market-clearing prices" are, as we have seen, compatible with the accumulation of inventories when investment in this form is judged to be the most profitable form of replacement or net accumulation at any moment, provided there is no monopolistic abuse (i.e., no exclusion of potentially competing resources from any area, occupation or firm).

of society's co-ordinative institutions) merely reduces particular market-clearing prices at any point of time. Moreover, the *initial* price cuts needed to set the recovery process going in any sector are, in each instance, *raising the market-clearing levels of prices in non-competing activities.* This is a vitally important point to which we must return (*see* Chap. XI, pp. 82-86). Say's law explains how, even if, in an attempt to escape from depression, institutions were deliberately designed to facilitate the appropriate pricing, the path to full utilization of productive capacity would be likely to involve some passage of time (simply because people happen to be as we know them to be). The crucial point is, however, that market-clearing prices will always be possible for all valuable inputs and outputs; and if incentives can be created for such pricing, some inputs and outputs which have been merely *potentially* valuable will become presently valuable.

In practice this implies that "full" or even something nearer to "optimal" utilization of all valuable services (of men and assets) can be envisaged as attainable unless, for political reasons, private duress or collusion in the fixing of wage-rates and prices is permitted. Inevitable inertias alone will, subject to considerations raised in Chapter XIII, merely slow down such achievements.

It is, however, essential to stress once again that even if, in a drastic attempt to escape from the chronic dilemma of depression or inflation and yet avoid the determination of prices for the private profit of politicians engaged in vote acquisition (as under "incomes policies"), institutions were deliberately designed to bring private duress in the pricing process to an end (by releasing incentives for the determination of market-clearing prices) *the automatic tendency to depression which Say's law exposes* could hardly be wholly eliminated. There would always be defects in the drafting of the required legislation, as well as error in enforcement by officials and judicial interpretations. It can be claimed, however, that the greater the success actually achieved in causing input and output prices to be fixed as closely as practicable to the prospective market-clearing level, the smaller will be the proportion of *waste* (unintended consumption), including that due to the idleness or idling of men and assets with their depressive consequences.

1. H. Neisser, "General Overproduction," in *Readings in Business Cycle Theory*, p. 387.
2. *Ibid.*, p. 390.
3. Keynes, *General Theory*, p. 26.
4. F. Quesnay, "Dialogue sur le Commerce" in *Les Physiocrates*, Ed., M. Daire, Part I, p. 170.
5. H. Neisser, *op. cit.*, p. 385; O. Lange, *Studies in Mathematical Economics*, pp. 57-61.
6. T. Sowell, *Say's Law*, p. 60.

V

THE CONCEPT OF WITHHOLDING

Some critical readers may still be unhappy about the concept of "withholding supplies." Given my insistence that a producer's decision to accumulate part of the output of his efforts and assets (or perhaps the whole of his output) is "actual demand" by him for that output, as well as its "actual supply," how can such "actual supplies" be clearly distinguished from "withheld supplies"? If inventories may pile up without "withholding," how can we recognize the circumstances in which "withholding" does occur?

To illustrate the issue, let us consider the case in which the *entrepreneur* is confronted with what he interprets as a *temporary* falling-off in demand for his products. *If his interpretation is correct*, market-clearing prices will have been compatible with his accumulating inventories. He will have made a profitable investment in the stockpile.

Suppose, however, that the entrepreneur's forecast is unduly optimistic. He will have been inadvertently holding back supplies and asking prices which exceed the market-clearing level.

Or suppose that accumulating inventories are accompanied by reduced supplies of and higher prices for inputs; and that the explanation is *not* that the input suppliers have raised their demands because other, more profitable outlets for their activities have successfully competed for their services, but that, acting in collusion, they have simply agreed to price their inputs higher. In those circumstances also, what I have termed "withholding" *must* be occurring. The explanation can be, then, either that potential input suppliers are asking more than "market-clearing input prices" or that entrepreneurs are doing so for their residual claim—their contribution to the creation of value.

Again, when demand for one type of output shrinks because, at current prices, the public prefers other things, and the change of preference is forecast as more or less permanent, then *ceteris paribus* "market-clearing prices" both for the inputs and the outputs must decline, creating thereby the required inducements for co-ordinative adjustments in resource use; the more promptly and successfully such adjustments occur, the smaller will be the proportion by which market-clearing prices must fall; and this is a matter of (a) the versatility and mobility of men and assets and (b) in the actual world, of the ability to lower or circumvent *man-made obstacles* to versatility and mobility, including politically imposed barriers.

All contractions in any particular flow of productive services, including the "marketing" services provided by inventories, whether due to deliberate "withholding" or not, will, unless countervailed by expansions of input and output flows elsewhere in the economy, tend to be "depressive" on non-competing activities (in the sense that all unreplaced consumption is depressive). In the instance considered before, in which an entrepreneur confronted with a decline in the demand for a commodity at the unchanged prices he is maintaining, continues to invest in the inputs (labor, materials, etc.), and to accumulate inventories of final products, because he expects

44

demand to recover, it *may*, as I have said, turn out to have been an inadvertent "withholding" and hence "depressive." It will prove to have been so if his expectations are *not* fulfilled; for in that case, market-clearing prices for the accumulating goods will have been unintendedly exceeded. But stockpiling of "end products," due to such wrong (inefficient or unlucky) forecasting is highly unlikely ever to be *important*. Moreover, if it does occur, the errors can be rapidly rectified, while continued misjudgments will be penalized (through market sanctions).

But neither speculative investment in inventories (the production of "time utilities") nor the provision of other marketing services (that is, the production of "availability" and "assembly" utilities) are "withholding." Inventories of all kinds (including money) are *normally* active capital. Their provision is demanded by and remunerated by the community in their consumer role. Only in the case of deliberate scarcity contrivance or entrepreneurial error will "withholding" occur. As I put it in my *Theory of Idle Resources, withheld* capacity is "idle," while stockpiles *may* be in "*pseudo*-idleness."

VI

UNEMPLOYMENT DISEQUILIBRIUM

Modern economists dealing with the topic we are discussing seem to find inspiration in Leon Walras' *Elements*. That they still have doubts or reservations about Say's law is puzzling to me because Walras' famous work can be reasonably interpreted as a detailed, mathematical statement of the law of markets, although Walras himself *seems* not to have perceived it. His exposition demonstrates, through the medium of a series of simultaneous equations, the interdependence and mutual determination of all values (prices). It shows further the function of such values established in allocating men and other resources to supplying different products. He conceived of this occurring through entrepreneurial "groping"—the setting of prices, and the reacting to prices set, *via* what Adam Smith called "the higgling of the market." In my own terminology, Walras showed that the amounts supplied (and hence demanded) of particular inputs and outputs were determined by the prices asked; while these prices were in turn influenced by the prices and hence the magnitudes of *other* inputs and outputs. Had he used the word "noncompeting" for "other," he would have greatly

46

clarified his message. But what he was demonstrating did not require the assumption of perfect price (and wage-rate) flexibility, as he seemed to think it did. The market-clearing prices for any particular kind of output (say cabbages) are influenced by the actual prices (whether rigid or flexible) of all the *other* things which contribute to the source of demands as a whole and hence influence (in the Walrasian conception, but expressed in my own terminology) demand for any particular thing —cabbages.

Walras explained *inter alia* that disequilibrium—a condition in which values in different parts of the economy are mutually inconsistent—sets in motion the "groping" efforts he envisaged at achieving consistency—a chain of price and contract revisions which mark the path to equilibrium. He described the process as "the mechanism of competition"[*][1]; and his analysis means that, if competition prevails, i.e., if the "groping" process is not suppressed (so that prices are not prevented from being adjusted in the manner required), not only full utilization of capacity (of men and assets) will be achieved but, subject to the considerations I raise in Chap. XIII, pp. 103-108, optimal utilization.

I have referred already to Walras' "identity." He seems, however, to have been showing (a) that the aggregate money value of sales must be identically equal to the aggregate money value of purchases—a wholly truistical proposition—and (b) that, on the assumption that an individual is not (in my terminology) investing in or disinvesting from money, and not himself investing in the final commodities he produces, the money value of his production must equal the money value of his purchases, *irrespective of any constraints on "the mechanism of free competition."* No person will be able to purchase an additional $x worth of goods or services unless he

---

[*]Sometimes he spoke of "free" competition and at other times of "market" competition.

has sold additional goods or services of this value, or unless he can borrow an equivalent money's worth from some other producer. And in this form the proposition is much less of a truism. It is an important implication of the law of markets.

In Chapter IV, p. 33, I asserted that the root co-ordinative act which keeps the economy in activity is the action of would-be sellers in pricing their inputs or outputs so as to permit sale of all services and products which are not retained by their producers for their own consumption or for investment in their own inventories (or, alternatively, in accepting would-be buyers' offers.) It is this last truth which some of those very critics of Keynes who have helped to expose the untenability of the unemployment equilibrium notion still seem hesitant to accept. I think particularly of Clower and Leijonhufvud, who appear to believe that certain at least of Keynes' innovations remain valid and relevant provided we think of unemployment *disequilibrium* instead of unemployment *equilibrium.*[*] The disequilibria which obviously exist in different parts of the economy, it is suggested, cannot be explained by traditional equilibrium analysis. Prior to Keynes, the implication is, economists could not fully account for the idleness of resources being regarded at times as more profitable than (or preferable to) their utilization. Still less could the "orthodoxy" of the 1920s account for *cumulative* contractions of activity.

Well, of course, *every* state of disequilibrium means that buying and/or selling take place with smaller inputs and outputs than would have been realized under equilibrium. This is a tenet of pure orthodoxy (*See* Chapter XI, p. 81), although Clower believes he is indicating something which the "orthodox" economists did not understand. He says: " . . . not every household can buy and sell just what it pleases if supply exceeds demand some-

---

[*]Patinkin was the first to take this line. Yeager more or less accepts the Clower-Leijonhufvud position.

where in the economy."[2] But the only objection the old "orthodox" economists would have had to this assertion, if it means "somewhere in the economy prices are falling, so that the disappointed producers will be able to dispose of a smaller income than they had expected, in acquiring non-competing things," is that Clower's assertion is equally possible under imaginary general equilibrium! The true principle is that no household can *ever* "buy and sell just what it pleases"; for it is constrained always either by free-market inputs, outputs, and prices (whether the prices resulting reflect equilibrium or some position during movement towards it) *or* constrained by inputs, outputs and prices influenced by deliberate restraints on the free market. For instance, it makes no difference whether the price of bricks is rising because an earthquake has increased the cost of getting the materials, or a cartel has limited supplies, or a strike threat has pushed up costs. The consequences are identical. *

Unemployment disequilibrium envisaged as an enduring condition of part of the potential labor force merely means that there are wage-rates determined by sheer inertia, legal enactment, official edict or private duress at levels above the market-clearing "equilibrium" for labor's inputs—the intersection of the relevant demand and supply schedules, while the laid-off resources (men and complementary assets), cheapened for other uses, have not yet found sub-optimal employments, i.e., not yet been absorbed into *the next best* utilizations. But in all cases of lasting divergencies from the equilibrium (whether above or below), quantities actually transacted (supplies and hence demands) are caused to contract. * That is, all disequilibria cause some re-

---

*Clower goes on to say that "the demand functions of orthodox theory do not provide relevant market signals."[2] That is, however, an important but quite different point, to which we shall have to return.

*See, pp. 28-29, 48-49, 81.

sources (men and assets) to become idle or idling *in the short run*; and, if the disequilibria are enduring, they cause the diversion of resources into less productive utilization (sub-optimal employment) *in the long run*. (The reasons why, in practice, the short-run may become indefinitely extended and create the phenomenon of *chronic* idleness are discussed in Chap. XIII, pp. 103-8. The vital reality implied by Say's law is that *every relaxation of the constraints through which market pressures to equilibrium are resisted* (e.g., as by costs and prices imposed by law, collusion or duress) *renders larger outputs profitably producible and hence makes larger non-competing outputs profitable.*

It is for this reason that I cannot accept Clower's suggestion that "orthodox analysis does not provide a general theory of disequilibrium states."[3]* I shall here be maintaining, on the contrary, that unless Say's law can still be shown to be defective, it provides a very clear, very simple and *completely general* theory to account for "unemployment *dis*equilibrium."

The failure of Keynesians and some of the critics of Keynesian economics to perceive the all-embracing significance of Say's law is largely due, I think, to the inherently defective concept of "aggregate demand" (not a purely Keynesian notion), which dictates their approach. Say was dealing with *demands in general—a complex of separate phenomena of preference which are incapable of any meaningful aggregation.* The demand for a particular productive service or commodity is merely *the value* (which *may* be and usually *is* measured in money, and effected through the use of money) *of whatever other services, or assets originating or existing somewhere else in the economy are happening*

---

*Clower's case is that orthodox economics "yields no direct information about the magnitude of *realized* as distinct from *planned* transactions under equilibrium conditions".[4] But realized data—prices and quantities—are not the only data from which decision-makers extrapolate; and every forecast is provisional, subject to continuous revision until the revised and the realized meet.

to be offered and exchanged for it. Attempts to add together all demands (or all supplies) to form "demand in general" (or "supply in general") are futile.

But the aggregate stock of assets and the number of people of working-age, with the corresponding services they provide, may be legitimately regarded as *the source of demands* (or of supplies). If the value of the flow of such services is what is meant by the term "aggregate demand," and the meaning is obvious to all readers, my point is merely a semantic one. It concerns appropriateness, that is all. But then the meaning of "aggregate demand" will be identical with that of "aggregate supply," and identical with "real income" as well. There can be no *schedule* of aggregate demand set against a schedule of aggregate supply when terms are used in this connotation; for each actual demand *is* an actual supply.

Much of the controversy could, I often think, be finally settled for all time if economists would only use terms as closely as possible in their ordinary, every-day connotations (which would seldom entail any sacrifice of rigor). Surely a demand is only "effective" when the demander gets what he wants in return for his offer to buy at a particular price or when he finds somewhere an offer to sell something he wants at a price which causes him to prefer it to the alternatives he has. And surely a supply is only "effective" when whoever offers something for sale at a particular price achieves a sale. If this commonsense principle is accepted, then obviously every "effective demand" *is* an "effective supply". *

Recognition of the point I am making in no way hinders our understanding of Walras' meticulous analysis of demand and supply in lessons 5 and 6 of his *Elements*, although (to distinguish mere "want", "desire" or "need" from an ability to offer or command money's worth in

---

*But a better term for "effective" in this connotation is "actual," as distinct from "potential" or "possible."

exchange) he used the term "effective" for offers to buy and offers to sell which might induce no transaction until (*via* the groping process) one party or the other, or both parties, changed the terms appropriately.[5]

We are now in a position to consider further the light which Say's law can throw upon the dynamics of recovery from recession. The following chapter is devoted to this topic.

1. Leon Walras, *Elements of Pure Economics*, A.E.A. translation, Irwin, 1954, p. 86.
2. R. W. Clower, *Monetary Theory*, p. 286.
3. *Ibid.*, p. 287.
4. *Ibid.*, p. 275.
5. Walras, *op. cit.*, pp. 83-91.

VII

THE TRUE MULTIPLIER

The cumulative decline in real income which is set up through any one contraction of supply not offset by another expansion of supply will, at each successive *induced* withholding of supplies (induced through rigidity of prices in noncompeting activities) tend to have a smaller effect. An eventual "equilibrium" (or "stable disequilibrium"*) will be reached at lower real income, probably with much "idle" or "idling" productive capacity (i.e., much unemployment) but possibly with much "suboptimal employment." That reaction chain is, I suggest, the negative operation of what I shall call *the true* or *real multiplier*. The reasons in this case are unconnected with the *Keynesian multiplier* thesis, *which depends upon "expenditures"—changes in the ownership of money.* Indeed, this view of the emergence of a chronic depression situation is the direct opposite of the Keynesian view of

---

*"Stable" in the sense of *unlikely to be disturbed* (a) by government action to protect incentives (loss-avoiding, profit-seeking) for the substitutions we call "competition" (*see* definition in Chap. II, p. 15), or (b) by successful competitive initiatives in spite of the absence of official action to dissolve duress-imposed costs or prices.

"unemployment equilibrium"; for under the conditions I have imagined, any market-pressured price cut, i.e., any increased supply, will tend to initiate a positive "real multiplier" effect—a cumulative rise in activity and real income, whereas Keynes' thesis is that price-cutting is self-frustrating, tending to aggravate the contraction of activities.

Yet the cumulative reaction which Say's law implies is almost exactly what Leijonhufvud is now treating as the Keynesian multiplier. He says:

> During the time that the individual searches for a new job, he is "unemployed" in the everyday sense of the word. Keynes' multiplier is based on the assumption that *the loss of receipts from current sales of labor services during this period will make him reduce his spending on consumer goods.* This second-round reduction in effective demand will cause additional unemployment, a consequent third-round reduction in demand, etc. Each successive increment to unemployment and decrement in aggregate demand will be smaller than the last, so there will be a limit to the total decline in income consequent upon an initial reduction in expenditures of given magnitude. But the process entails an *amplification* of the initial deflationary disturbance.[1]

[The italics in the text are mine.] What *should* have been said in the words italicized is, I suggest: " . . . the loss of some workers' inputs during this period will reduce those workers' contribution to the source of demands for all non-competing inputs."

Let us consider first the last sentence of Leijonhufvud's quotation. The initiating "disturbance" need not have been *deflationary* in the sense of *monetary* deflation. That is solely a matter of monetary policy. Under monetary flexibility and price rigidity, *any* new withholding of capacity (the pricing of additional potential productive services above market-clearing levels—beyond the reach of current income—as judged by entrepreneurs) will tend to set going the consequences to which Leijonhufvud refers.

Hence it is certainly possible to *imagine* the state of affairs he describes, under which productive capacity (of men and assets) becomes *chronically priced for under-utilization,* with the flow of wages and income subject at first to a self-aggravating contraction and later to a relatively stable condition of sub-optimal utilization of men and assets. But the assumption then is that, through inertias, collusive action or otherwise, the pricing system—the market-clearing system—is restrained. *There is "equilibrium" (or "stable disequilibrium") only in the sense that market pressures to restore fuller or more productive activity are suppressed.*

Such a situation is aggravated if income transfers are used to subsidize the idleness (e.g., as through "unemployment compensation" or "price supports"). The "unemployment" then becomes a collectively purchased product, similar in effect to private decisions in favor of greater leisure. There is indeed "unemployment equilibrium" in a special sense—chronic unemployment. Far from negating Say's law, however, such a situation is *explained by* that law; for as I suggested above, if wage-rate cuts and price cuts *could* occur, they would be capable (in the circumstances imagined) of initiating a "multiplier" effect, restoring the wages-flow and the income-flow. It follows that an understanding of Say's law is essential not only for any realistic insight into the nature and genesis of depression (depression being brought about by a succession of withdrawals of supplies, which is a succession of withdrawals of demands), but of chronic unemployment due to subsidization of the condition by income transfers, or of the "sub-optimal full employment" which must eventually result in the absence of subsidized idleness.

I must stress that the "sub-optimal full employment" condition* differs fundamentally from that of *chronic unemployment,* in the ordinary connotation of that term.

---

*Joan Robinson has described what I have called "sub-optimal full employment" as "disguised unemployment". In my *Theory of Idle Resources,* I called it "diverted capacity" (as distinct from "withheld capacity").

It seems to me that, if it were not for various ways in which idleness is subsidized, unemployment could not long persist. "Waste" would continue, and it could well be chronic waste, but productive resources would find other, less productive and less remunerative employments. The composition of the stock of assets would adapt itself, while displaced workers, and juveniles reaching working-age, would enter new or different occupations. When all resources (men and assets) were employed in that manner, there would be "full employment"—although "sub-optimal employment." I shall return to this point, which I regard as vital.

In Leijonhufvud's interpretation, it is the fact—explicitly asserted—that "goods are always exchanged for *money* and money for goods"[2] which is diagnosed as the crucial explanation of the phenomenon that Keynes thought he had discerned. But why should the use of the monetary mechanism be conducive to the discoordination of the economy? Why should it precipitate a disorder which may be manifested in growing layoffs of labor, with productive capacity being thrown into cumulatively worsening idleness, following an initial stimulus? Why should the fact that market institutions are served by a measuring rod of value be held responsible, at times, for causing initially valuable (because initially demanded) productive resources (men and assets) to drift into unproductiveness, temporary idleness, and, with the assistance of income transfers, into chronic idleness? The following chapter will consider whether the use of money is in any way likely to disconnect one supplier and demander from other suppliers and demanders, thereby inaugurating or perpetuating depression.

1. Leijonhufvud, *Keynes and the Classics*, (London, Institute of Economic Affairs, 1969), p. 32.
2. *Ibid*, p. 33.

VIII

THE ALLEGED HIATUS

There *is* a sense in which the use of money *appears* to be partly responsible for the phenomenon which Clower has recently termed "the dual-decision" situation (although the appearance is, I shall suggest, illusory). In my own terminology, Clower is concerned with a condition of the economy in which *potential decisions to consume* and *potential decisions to produce* do not connect, or under which *potential decisions to work and potential decisions to employ* do not connect. The rate of extermination of value and the rate of replacement of value both shrink, leaving a stable disequilibrium of idle or idling productive capacity. We should notice that the condition envisaged is one which was broadly perceived and thought about before the Keynesian era. The explanation of it is not, I shall maintain, that which Clower has in mind. Nor does it accord with the theories of Leijonhufvud and Patinkin about the responsibility of money for a hiatus between workers and intermediaries.

I can illustrate by Cannan's treatment of the situation in 1933. Making the point that, in a co-operative world, people would not be able to sell their services or outputs if they asked "terms which the rest did not think good enough to be accepted . . .", i.e., "if they persisted in asking more . . . than the consumers, potential and actual, of the product of that labor thought it was worth,"[1] he stressed the practical difficulty of getting the implications of this simple truth understood. He said, to talk of " . . . the workers of the world as having arranged terms on which to work for each other, certainly *seems* a little unreal . . . "[2] (although, he said, that was indeed what happened). In the actual world most persons "are employed by intermediaries"; hence, he said, "unemployment is likely to be somewhat greater. . . . When a person is offering services to an employer who resells to the consumers, it is much less obvious to him that in order to keep employment he must produce what the consumer wants at a price which the consumer will pay."[3] The worker is therefore naturally likely to give too little weight to the fact that the amounts which it will be profitable to produce and sell of the things into which his labor is embodied will diminish as costs rise. "General unemployment appears when asking too much is a general phenomenon. . . . " Moreover, "when nearly all bargains are made in terms of money, and incomes are universally reckoned in money, general illusion is easier and disillusionment is unlikely to come so quickly. When A and B, instead of exchanging their products directly, both sell them in the market and do not come face to face, their extravagant pretensions are not confronted with each other."[4]

Although Cannan mentioned the significance of the intermediary, he did not envisage any hiatus between the worker and the intermediary, as in Clower's and Leijonhufvud's exposition, but that between worker and worker. Yet Cannan was drawing attention, I feel, to a vastly more important aspect of reality than the phenomenon of unjustified entrepreneurial pessimism which is, as we shall see, so important in Leijonhufvud's and Clower's discussion. What both of these economists regard as a failure of communications—a failure of market signals—is really between worker and worker, and entrepreneur and entrepreneur (or between entrepreneur *plus* workers in one field and entrepreneur *plus* workers in non-competing fields) rather than between the worker and the entrepreneur intermediary who risks investment in the worker's labor.

I suggest, however, that it is *not* mainly through "the money illusion," and the facts that "bargains are made in money" and "incomes universally reckoned in money" that the difficulties to be overcome originate, as Cannan suggested. *The hiatus arises owing to that remoteness of wage-earner and wage-earner, and of entrepreneur and entrepreneur, which is an inevitable consequence of the highly efficient but highly complex system of division of labor that money and the pricing system make possible.* Except in this sense, *the use of money has nothing whatsoever to do with the problem. The remoteness of producer and consumer* is relevant but less important *in this context.* *

Of course, inflation and purposeless deflation are relevant. But they are *diseases of money* not the *use of money.* And admittedly both monetary policy and pricing policy must take the "money illusion" into account. But the weakness to which Cannan was referring can be eradicated, not by monetary reform but by reform of the pricing system—mainly to protect the workers from what Cannan called their own "extravagant" and hence ruinous "pretensions."

The use of money can be held only to facilitate, never frustrate, the process of asking market-clearing exchange values, i.e., values which permit a better (a fuller) utilization of productive capacity. But Leijonhufvud's stress on the *medium of exchange* seems to reinforce his assumption that, under hypothetical barter, the problems created by the power to withhold productive capacity would be non-existent.

---

*It is of the greatest importance in another context. *See* Chapter VI of my book, *The Strike-Threat System*, entitled "The Employer Stereotype".

There seems to be no reason, however, why barter should release incentives for the asking of market-clearing values. Unless we assume *perfect value flexibility in an imaginary barter economy of assumed equal complexity,* all the phenomena encountered under imperfect price flexibility will have to be assumed to influence adversely the incentives to co-ordinated activity. Under such assumptions, there will be no mitigation of the *remoteness* between a worker in one industry and a worker in another, or between entrepreneurs in one industry and those in others.

Surely the use of money not only solves the difficulties due to the absence of "double coincidence of wants" but *enormously* eases the process of adjusting the values (prices) demanded for things offered or the values (prices) offered for things demanded (in response to changes in preference or changes in supply conditions). The use of money tends to minimize the likelihood of entrepreneurial error, and helps *to ensure that input and output flows shall be continuous even under the complexities of the highly advanced division of labor which the monetary mechanism has rendered possible.* This is indeed the justification for the ancient insight which described the task of money as that of a *lubricant.* But ease of adjustment does not necessarily mean *will to adjust,* particularly in a society which permits duress-imposed wage-rates, or other forms of scarcity contrivance.

1. Cannan, *Economic Scares,* (London, P. S. King, 1933), p. 31.
2. *Ibid.,* pp. 31-2
3. *Ibid.,* p. 35.
4. *Ibid.,* p. 38.

IX

YEAGER'S INTERPRETATION

In a very interesting paper, published since the present book was submitted to the publisher, Leland B. Yeager suggests that basically my position does not differ from that of Leijonhufvud and Clower. Nevertheless, he thinks that the crux of their insights lies in their recognition of the fact that "money alone among all assets, has no price of its own and no market of its own".[1] I feel myself, however, that the expositions of all three economists mentioned are clouded by this conviction about the special nature of money. The fact that prices are values expressed in terms of money, so that the money unit cannot have "a *price* of its own," does not prevent the money unit from having "a *value* of its own." And the value of the money unit is market-determined,* even when its value is defined in a monetary ("convertibility") obligation. Under any monetary standard, it is the contractual duty* of the

---

*Edwin Cannan made this clear as early as 1921 in his *Economic Journal* article, "The Application of the Theoretical Apparatus of Supply and Demand to Units of Currency."

*The contractual obligation is of course not only with those who hold money but with all who make their own plans and conclude their own contracts in money terms.

61

monetary authority to control the "supply" of money units in order to maintain a stipulated market value for the "container" of purchasing power. (*See* pp. 21-22).

The demand for money arises from the positions which monetary services occupy on peoples' scales of preference and/or their judgment of the productivity of those services. It is this demand which determines the aggregate real value of money; while the "money supply," the number of money units—the number of "containers" in which, so to speak, that aggregate real value is divided—is determined by monetary policy.* I do not understand why Yeager thinks that these factors, which determine the size of the measuring rod, induce income constraints in the form of the withholding of supplies and hence of demands, except in the sense that, in the presence of downward cost and price rigidities, deflation will aggravate the cumulative withholding process—just as *unanticipated* inflation will mitigate or reverse it.

It is no valid objection to this thesis to say that "demands" may originate, not in "supplies", but in "newly created" or "newly activated" money. For inflations* or deflations *which do not (via price-cost reactions) affect the magnitudes of "supplies,"* do not affect the magnitude of the source of "demands": they merely dilute or condense it: they do not cause aggregate *purchasing power* to expand or contract but merely cause aggregate *money-spending power* to expand or contract.* Thus, in the course of an inflation

---

*The acceptance of a monetary standard, such as the gold standard, simply limits the discretionary element in monetary policy.

*Including those caused by "monetary rigidity", i.e., as when monetary policy ignores a declining demand for money—i.e., ignores "new activation" of money.

*See pp. 18-19, 118-119.

62

each money unit contains a diminishing purchasing power.*
A forger does not contribute to the source of demands.
He steals someone else's *supplies* (whatever he buys
with the forged money) because he has stolen their demands.

Some of Keynes' critics have followed him in perpetuating the notion that "supplies" of non-money must
be viewed, not as contributions to "aggregate demand,"
but as contributions to the demand for money. It is true
of course that any increase in "supplies" (a rise in the
real GNP) implies *ceteris paribus* a proportional rise
in demand for monetary services. But as I shall be
stressing almost *ad nauseam*, the flows of productive
services ("supplies"—non-monetary or monetary) are
expressions of demands for non-competing "supplies"
as a whole; and although these non-competing productive
services demanded *include* monetary services as inputs
(or, for consumers, as outputs), *non-money services
make up by far the greater proportion in the aggregate.*
The phenomenon of selling no more contributes to the
demand for money than the phenomenon of buying supplies
money. That is, "the money supply" being assumed
constant, selling and buying do not bid down or bid up
the value of the money unit *unless, on balance, people
plan to allow their money inventories to run down or plan
to accumulate money inventories respectively.* And then
it is entirely a question of changing preferences or
changing entrepreneurial judgment of relative productivity
in respect of money and non-money. (Whether these
preferences or judgments are influenced by "illusion"
in some measure is irrelevant. In any case, all our
preferences and judgments are so influenced!)

*There are also real income transfers (a) from contractual claimants on the
value of output to residual claimants, or (b) from those whose money incomes
rise less than the average to those whose money incomes rise more than the
average, or (c) from creditors to debtors, or (d) from the ruled to the rulers.
How such income transfers influence the source of demands is not an issue
in the present context. (But *see* pp. 121-123).

Leland Yeager, referring to my exposition of this topic in my *Keynesianism*, suggests that my theory "is incomplete" because I do not "show how an adequate money supply keeps non-monetary disturbances from causing cumulative deterioration." He says that I do not put "the blame for such deterioration on money in particular".[2] It is indeed true that I do not "blame" money, or rather the failure to *spend* money, for the generation of depression; but I do recognize all the reactions that Yeager has in mind when he thinks of the money supply being raised to an "adequate" volume. Unanticipated inflation *is* a way, albeit a very crude way, of mitigating incipient depression. And when economists think and talk of "a money supply compatible with full employment," or of "the optimal rate of inflation," or (like Yeager) of "an adequate money supply," they are really envisaging the process under which "supplies" (and hence "demands") withheld through pricing can be restored by an unanticipated contraction of the measuring-rod of money. *

The "monetarists" think in terms of an *"adequate" money supply* which can at any rate assist in maintaining the continuity of the market-clearing process while pure "Keynesians" say that it is an *"adequate" rate of spending* that matters. But the crucial continuity is *always* dependent upon valuing and pricing, whether or not monetary policy is flexible, rigid, inflationary or deflationary—i.e., independently of the factors which determine the purchasing power of the money unit. Certainly some monetary policies facilitate the process—at a cost—while others make it more difficult.

---

*Thus, a central bank, taking into account a careful judgment about the effectiveness with which the public can be misled concerning the speed and duration of any inflation planned, can cause prospective yields to rise (a reduction of input costs in relation to output prices occurring through the depreciation of the money unit).

It will help to clarify the issue if we consider the significance of spending. Given any "money supply," it is the demand for money to hold (not to spend) which determines the value of the money unit; and given the demand for money to hold, it is monetary policy which, in determining the "money supply," determines the value of the unit. Spending is incidental. If prices in general rise, then in such transactions as must be made through spending, an increased number of money units must be offered for any *quantum* of non-money. Each price established represents what must be spent if a good is to be *sold and purchased*. The increased spending is, then, a consequence not a cause. It is the valuing process, not the spending (which *follows* the valuing) that determines prices. The truth of this proposition is established by the fact that all present prices are influenced by expectations of future prices. Another proof is that the prices of goods often change in a market which is closed for a period during which no spending on the goods could have occurred!

1. L. B. Yeager, "The Keynesian Diversion," *Western Economic Journal*, June, 1973, p. 151.
2. *Ibid.*, p. 159.

X

"EFFECTIVE DEMAND" IN RELATION TO SAVING PREFERENCE AND LIQUIDITY PREFERENCE

It is puzzling to me that such acute critics of Keynes as Leijonhufvud, Clower and Yeager still seem not to have shaken off the notion (expressed in my terminology) that some supplies of non-money do not become "effective" demands because, in the aggregate, sellers demand (temporarily) additional money instead of other non-money; or, as it is sometimes expressed, that conditions can arise in which an "excess demand" for money can develop—an "excess" which (in Keynes' words) can be "choked off" only by depression and unemployment. In such circumstances, it is held, "aggregate demand" becomes "deficient" (some portion of that demand being "ineffective").

For example, using Keynes' phrases from his *Treatise on Money* (1930) and not from the *General Theory*, following him in linking saving preference with liquidity preference, and stating that *savers* want "wealth as such," described as "the potentiality of *consuming* an unspecified article at an unspecified time,"* Leijonhufvud

*The reference to consumption here is not easily interpreted. Of course the ultimate purpose of *all* economic activity is consumption. But one is more likely to invest in money *temporarily* in order later to acquire assets which are expected to yield an income-stream (i.e. long-life assets—producer goods) than for the purpose of acquiring short-life assets (consumer goods) or services.

appears to think that Say's law is upset, and enduring unemployment *dis*equilibrium is made possible because, on occasion, *savers* (*see* my definition, p. 16) invest in additional money rather than in non-money.[1]

But non-savers or even dissavers may also want to acquire "unspecified things at unspecified times" to a greater extent than previously and so increase their holdings of money or the proportion of money in their total assets. In general demands for the services of money are independent of the saving process.

The general notion that I am questioning seems to be that some demands are "ineffective" because they are not expressed through the offer of money. We have seen, however, that a self-employed farmer may, *without purchasing*, demand and consume the inputs of his own labor and those of his equipment.* But the real point at issue is surely that when a person. buys, he normally demands with *money's worth*, not with money. He demands with money only when he happens to be reducing his investment in it (i.e., not concurrently replenishing his money holdings), *for he can always obtain money costlessly by realizing his inputs or outputs (services or assets) at their money's worth.* (An awareness of my definitions of "money's worth," "market-clearing price," pp. 19-20, and "withheld capacity", 20-21, as well as my further explanation of these concepts in Chapter V, is, I think, essential for a full understanding of this and the following paragraph). I say that he *can*; but it may not be profitable for him to do so; for the market-clearing price of the full output of a thing exceeds money's worth when *investment in inventories* of it promises yields in excess of interest. The reader is reminded that, when a person is asking more' than the money's worth of the whole output of what he and his assets produce, he may be regarded as investing in the output; while if he asks more than the market-clearing value, then he is withholding

---

*Walras suggested that such a person should be regarded as two persons, one who invests in the equipment and one who consumes its services.

supply and contributing to the cumulative contraction of activity that we have been considering.

The holding of money is not costless. Just as with all other assets held, interest is a cost. And money is productive. The incentives to invest in it (as I stressed above) are no different from those for investment in non-money assets, with the ever-present possibility of speculative gain or loss to supplement or detract from the non-speculative yield. *It is the acquisition and spending of money which is costless.* It follows that money is as incidental (and as important) as cash registers and cashiers in the demanding and supplying process. I hope that, in stressing this truth (which the pre-Keynesian economists understood), I shall not be accused of attempting to explain "monetary phenomena by real causes." (*See* pp. 110-111).

Leijonhufvud's repeated references to "purchasing power" stress the implication I am challenging, namely, that *the use of money* to pay for labor's inputs somehow either prevents those inputs from being supplied, or *if supplied*, from being an effective contribution to demands for non-competing things. I have been unable to find any satisfactory explanation of why the need for a temporary depletion of money stocks in the course of paying for labor, or the need for the replenishment of money stocks (as with other inventories) in order to be in a position to pay for labor at the next payday, can either frustrate the will to supply labor, or reduce (or destroy) the profitableness of demanding labor. In short, I have discerned no reasons why the employment of the monetary mechanism should prevent *potential demands* for non-competing outputs from becoming *actual demands.*

The fact that people in general (savers, non-savers and dissavers) will at times judge money to become more desirable than previously relatively to non-money does not seem to me to be relevant. They will do so, of course, when they predict that *present* yields from investment in additional non-money assets are less favorable than *future* yields from non-money investments are destined to be; and this usually implies that they are expecting (a) downward cost adjustments, or (b) downward price adjustments, or (c) a rise in the market rate of interest at some time in the future. In the case of (a) and (b) we have the phenomenon of what I have called "unstable price or cost rigidities." And far from the market pressures exerted when speculative investment in liquidity is so induced being of an equilibrium-disturbing type, those pressures are *tending* to break through inertias, or other unstable barriers, and facilitate equilibrium.

Moreover, under any monetary standard of the commodity type (e.g., the gold standard), speculative demand for liquidity may supply an additional, deflationary compulsion for the price and wage-rate adjustments towards the market-clearing levels which alone can restore the wages and income flow. This does not mean that, at times, speculative investment in money may not over-correct, or that attempts to correct through a policy of "monetary flexibility" may never over-correct. But under effective monetary flexibility, although deflationary pressures to price adjustment will be avoided,* other pressures tending to break down barriers to recovery—unstable cost and price rigidities—will still build up (through the absence of hopes of any inflationary validation of unstably rigid costs). Such pressures will increase in force because it will become increasingly obvious that it is not in the interests of would-be wage earners or the owners of assets that their valuable (i.e.,

*A policy of "monetary flexibility" will permit the development of latent inflation as long as the demand for money is *abnormally* high, but the monetary authority will be committed to avoiding open inflation when the demand for money becomes normal, i.e., committed to allowing the "money supply" to run down as individual money holdings are reduced (M to decline as V increases) unless, of course, expansion of real income should happen to offset the inflationary tendency.

potentially demanded) productive capacity shall remain idle.

We can now return to Leijonhufvud's conviction (following Keynes) that recession is aggravated *inter alia* by provision for the future (saving) rising in people's scales of preference when activity declines *and* by the superiority of money as a store of value when this occurs. He assumes that the prospective productiveness of money increases, not for speculative reasons owing to downward cost rigidities (and price rigidities) being judged to be unstable, but for other reasons.

There are two separate questions raised here. *Firstly*, because the condition of recession implies a decline in real income or a decline in the rate of growth of real income, why *should* consumption in the distant future come to rise in scales of preference in relation to consumption in the immediate future? One would *expect* both the *absolute* aggregate value of the replacement of consumption and the *absolute* value of additions to the stock of assets to decline but with the latter declining *relatively;* for it is surely easier to postpone provision for the future than to postpone consumption. On the other hand, apprehensions of straitened circumstances might conceivably induce people in general to decide to save a larger proportion of a falling real income. *For the sake of argument, let us assume that they do.*

We are then brought back to the *second* question which we encountered earlier (pp. 67-69) Why should savers in particular (as distinct from other owners of assets) regard money as a superior store of value to non-money assets? Leijonhufvud's idea that savers "want wealth as such," in the sense of wanting "the potentiality of consuming an unspecified article at an unspecified time," does not explain why, for the time being, savers judge the productivity of money to rise relatively to the productivity of non-money: it is simply a way of asserting it. Leijonhufvud does not refer in this context to such factors as I have just mentioned.

70

It is true, of course that savers want "wealth as such." But *all* assets are wealth. *All* assets and not merely money are a "store of value." And while at times money may seem to be an exceptionally efficient store of value, at other times it is a prospectively poor store of value. As I have already insisted, all assets and services constitute *power to demand through buying* at their money's worth. (*See* definition, p. 19) But I can conceive of no reason why, (i) during periods of increasing thrift, or (ii) (a wholly separate issue) during recession, or (iii) during (i) and (ii) together, *the non-speculative prospective yield to money held* should rise relatively to yields to non-money.

The *non-speculative* prospective productivity of money held as a producer good will tend to fall, not rise, as profitable outputs decline. Inventories of money will not be fully replaced for the same reasons that inventories of materials will not be fully replaced in recession. Post-Keynesian economists seem to forget that the rate of interest is a cost of holding *all* assets. In my own confessedly heretical judgment, when the market rate of interest is abnormally low, the only reason why the relative productivity of money should increase is that *the probability of a rise in the rate of interest is then likely to be higher* and hence likely to induce *a speculative* increase in demand for money.

In the case of recession, only (a) downward cost and price rigidities judged to be unstable, or (b) deflation [which may temporarily aggravate the factors under (a)], or (c) a forecast rise in the rate of interest, can explain an increase in speculative demand for money which more than offsets the decline in non-speculative demand for it (due to the contraction of "supplies" in general). And even so, the bidding up of the aggregate real value of money for such reasons (or for any other imaginary reason, such as mere inertia in the acquisition of non-money while savings are increasing) need not be deflationary. *That is, one is not compelled to assume any particular monetary policy.*

71

The misconceptions which, I think, abound on this subject may be largely due to misleading terminology. If any portion of "aggregate demand" is described as "ineffective" when it is directed to money, in spite of the fact that the demander of money obtains "wealth as such" —assets equal in value to what he sells in order to invest in money—it is a most eccentric use of the term "ineffective," to say the least. The demander obtains what he demands! And when that portion of "aggregate demand" which is directed to money is simultaneously called "excess," it implies not only that that portion of demand *is* effective but that it is too effective! Then if so, what portion? The portion which *would* cause deflation under monetary rigidity? If that *is* the implication, why is it not expressed that way? An increase in the *relative* demand for money simply means that the aggregate real value of money rises relatively to the aggregate real value of non-money. But this is truistical. We do not say that some portion of the demand for rye is "ineffective" because some former purchasers of it demand wheat instead.

In Keynes' equations, M (the money supply) is constant. But this *explicit* assumption of monetary rigidity for expositional purposes tends not to be abandoned when policy conclusions are inferred; and in post-Keynesian economics, it often intrudes, I think, as a *tacit, implied assumption.* Yet it is fantastically unrealistic. For instance, what eventually became Keynes' *bête noire,* the pre-1914 gold standard, provided a very high degree of monetary flexibility. *

The real issues are, I suggest, most successfully clarified *under the opposite and less unrealistic assumption, namely, of perfect monetary flexibility.* Under "monetary flexibility," the money valuation of real income varies in proportion to real income. Hence no "gap" can arise

---

*Although, in a better system of government than the *pseudo*-democracy of the 20th century, the "orthodox" economists would have welcomed a system with an even higher flexibility. (*See* pp. 118-120, 128-132).

in "the stream of spending" except through the withholding of "supplies" and the consequential contraction of income. Yet under this imaginary condition recession, or even a serious depression can still develop. Typical prices of non-money (an appropriate price index) will not fall, *but an economy can run down just as it can under anticipated inflation.* Hence the notion of what I have called "the supply," as distinct from the "potential supply," of one thing becoming "ineffective" as a contribution to the source of demands for non-competing things (other than money) has no meaning. "Monetary flexibility" (in contrast to "price flexibility") alone is incapable of correcting the "automatic" process which throws men and assets into idleness.

The reality is, then, that depression can emerge only through *an interruption of the stream of "supplies,"* any interruption of the "stream of spending" being an effect—not a cause.* But if the "money supply"— the value of the money stock in terms of actual money units —is caused to lag in relation to an increase in the aggregate real value of that stock (the case of monetary rigidity) the scale of prices *must* fall and, under the additional assumption of widespread wage-rate and price rigidity, depression will be inevitable. In those circumstances, deflationary monetary policy, *not the use of money,* explains everything. Of course, periodic *rectifying* deflations (offsetting an unintended inflationary situation), i.e., what Leijonhufvud presumably means by "recurrent attacks of central bank perversity,"[3] must cause some avoidable dislocations and possible strains on the adjustment mechanism. *But any depressive consequences will still be due to the withholding of supplies.*

---

*In Leland Yeager's contribution to Clower's *Monetary Theory,* he accepted my reasoning on this point. In his paper, "The Keynesian Diversion",[2] however, he says he now thinks he "conceded too much to the non-monetary view of depression." But the latter view is truly the explanation of *all* depression. When deflation is the initiating factor (under downward cost or price rigidity), the economy still runs down through the cumulative consequences of the withdrawal of supplies of non-money.

The notion of demands being "ineffective" explains nothing.

When there is an "excess supply" of labor, says Leijonhufvud, "the offer of labor services (by the unemployed) does not constitute exercise of purchasing power over commodities, i.e., it does not constitute *effective* demand."[4]* "Workers find that their labor is not a source of direct purchasing power over output."[5] Well, admittedly, a worker's skills and muscle power do not become "purchasing power" (or barter power!) if they are priced (or valued) above the market-clearing level; and in this case that means *inconsistently with prospective yields from investment in them*; or, expressed somewhat differently, if they are not priced in conformity with the community's predicted ability to acquire the output, which includes the case in which they are priced inconsistently with price expectations. Labor is "supplied" only when the workers who offer it accept a wage-rate which entrepreneurs believe will return (through subsequent sale of the resulting output) not less than it has cost (the "means of payment" for it); then, *through the labor inputs supplied* and *the outputs into which they are embodied having been priced at their money's worth, they become "money-spending power"*; and if there has been (a) no monopolistic withholding of labor supplied, and (b) neither monopsonistic constraint in the purchase of labor's inputs nor monopolistic constraint in the pricing of the outputs, the money's worth of both inputs and outputs will have corresponded to their market-clearing prices.

Now the "constraints" to which I have just referred appear to be seen by Leijonhufvud as arising out of the

---

*Leijonhufvud's diagnosis of "ineffective demand" for, or "excess supply" of, labor as the chief condition that constrains demands for goods is influenced by and closely resembles Clower's diagnosis. But the former's treatment discloses more clearly what I feel is the core of the controversy and I have found it most fruitful therefore to direct my criticism mainly at Leijonhufvud's text.

process of depleting and replenishing money. Referring to "producers" (meaning the residual claimants on the value of outputs, and not the workers), he says they "find that their output is not a means of payment for the purchase of labor's inputs".[6] But while neither inputs nor outputs are money, they do have money's worth, which, *ceteris paribus*, will be higher the larger the potential supplies that are "withheld." And as I have already stressed, *at* their money's worth the exchange into money is costless, as is the subsequent exchange of money for a different form of non-money. There is, as I have insisted above, a cost of *holding* money, not a cost of *using* it to sell or buy.

Because all firms must sell their outputs in order to pay wages and settle debts, they would not have risked providing the fixed assets needed for the employment of workers unless they had been able to plan with confidence the replenishment of their money stocks as they met wages claims, just as they had planned also for replenishment of inventories of materials. That is, in a money economy, entrepreneurs try to proceed so as always to achieve a sufficient stock or flow of money's worth to settle all debts incurred, including those incurred with contractual claimants on the value of outputs, as well as to earn a residue and avoid losses.

It is equally obvious that *some of* the goods piling up in warehouses or shops will not be making their full potential contribution to the source of demands if they are being priced higher than is destined to induce their sale at the optimal rate, i.e., higher than will maximize the yield to the capital invested in them. What may be called "normal" inventories, at all stages of production, consist of goods of which the full production process is incomplete at the stage in question, because all the services demanded by potential customers (including the production of "availability utilities," "assembly utilities" and "time utilities") have 'not yet been incorporated into them. *Customers* demand "reserves" of non-

75

money and money—that is, they demand (and remunerate) the services of the capital invested in inventories as well as the fixed capital and the risk-bearing function. If allowance is made for this complication, it seems clear that services and goods are not "supplied," i.e., they do not enter into the source of demands, until (a) their owners invest in them for their own purposes* (in which case the owners both supply *and* demand them), or (b) ask *a value in exchange or price which induces exchange or purchase* (for investment or consumption). What needs to be explained is *why* some services and some goods should *not* be so valued or priced.

Leijonhufvud's continuation of the argument does not appear to me to clear up the difficulties. He says that because "workers ask for *money wages*, . . . from the standpoint of prospective employers . . . , the offer of labor services is not directly connected with a demand for additional output."[7] I am not sure of the exact meaning of the words, "not directly connected", or of the phrase, quoted before (p. 74), "labor is not a source of direct purchasing power over output." A firm taking on formerly unemployed workers will *usually* plan to invest *simultaneously* (a) in the services of this additional labor, (b) in additional inventories of materials and work in progress, (c) in additional inventories of money, and (d) (possibly) in additional fixed assets. And as the firm will thereby increase *its* output, it will be adding to the source of demands for additional outputs of non-competing producers *as its products are priced for clearance.* Moreover, it will know (or ought to know) that if firms in non-competing sectors of the economy are doing the same thing, there will be for that reason an *additional* justification for an increase in *its* output. General recovery in activity gives rise to general and justified entrepreneurial optimism. Such optimism will raise the wage-rates at which employment

---

*"Their own purposes" covers the intention to consume the goods. (*See* definition of "supply", pp. 14-15, 34.

76

for additional workers will be prospectively profitable. *But* less optimistic expectations will not mean that all workers wanting to be employed cannot supply their labor. At appropriately lower initial wage-costs, it will always be profitable to employ them unless their services are offered in a field in which they are completely valueless. I shall return to this point.

The surviving idea in post-Keynesian writings that the exercise of positive time preference is depressive does not always rest on the belief that the use of money creates a *hiatus*, but that the desire to provide for the future means a cessation of "demand". Because savers may not *now* know exactly how they will, at "some unspecified time", finally satisfy their time preference (i.e., choose the presently "unspecified" services or commodities they are destined ultimately to consume) *does not mean that they cease to demand current inputs and outputs*. A rise in saving-preference does not mean that savers' demands are postponed. It means that such demands are directed to different services and assets. Savers demand either (a) productive services of men and assets for embodiment into assets of different prospective lifespans, *or* (b) when, through this process, the costs of productive services have been bid up to a certain value, they demand existing assets (because investment in them offers, in prospect, a larger income stream).

1. Leijonhufvud, *Keynes and the Classics*, p. 37.
2. Yeager, "The Keynesian Diversion", *Western Economic Journal*, 1973, p. 8.
3. Leijonhufvud, *On Keynesian Economics and the Economics of Keynes*, New York, O.U.P., 1968, p. 399.
4. Leijonhufvud, *Keynes and the Classics*, p. 35.
5. *Ibid.*, p. 35.
6. *Ibid.*, p. 35.
7. *Ibid.*, p. 35.

XI

THE HIATUS—A DIFFERENT INTERPRETATION

In Clower's and Leijonhufvud's treatments, there is what I interpret as a quite different explanation suggested for "the hiatus"—an explanation which is independent of the demand for money issue, although neither economist recognizes this explicitly. Nevertheless, both are, I think, imagining here that entrepreneurs judge that, to sell enough of a product to make it profitable to employ all the potentially available labor for producing it, the output must be priced not below a certain value, with prospective labor costs not above a certain value, while the workers who constitute the additional "potentially available labor" for that activity find that, if they are to make their employment profitable for the entrepreneurs, and thereby acquire "purchasing power over output," *they must price their labor more cheaply than they are prepared (or permitted) to accept.* That is, the point may simply be that the workers are not in fact prompted *spontaneously* (or allowed) to make the adjustments needed and *actually supply* their labor. The condition of downward wage-rate rigidity may certainly be envisaged in this way. It is indeed exactly the point that Cannan made in 1933 (*see* pp. 57-59). But the main point at issue is this: If workers generally *are* persuaded to price their labor in relation to current *prospective* yields from investment in it, is there any reason why the process must be self-frustrating?

The phrase "excess supply of labor" (in a particular occupation or in occupations generally) is, so interpreted, merely an indirect way of saying that some workers are "unemployable" *at the wage-rates for which they are holding out.* In other words, the pricing of labor is inconsistent with prospectively profitable investment in the inputs of all those whose services would otherwise be available. Hence *what is usually called "unemployed labor" could be more realistically called "unsupplied labor"*; and any labor which remains "unsupplied" represents, because it is over-priced, *a withheld potential contribution to the source of demands for non-competing outputs.*

Just as the goods labor helps to replace, or to add to, are "supplied" only when they are priced for movement into the next stage of production or into business or household inventories, so is labor "supplied" only when it is priced so that entrepreneurs *expect* to be able to sell its contribution to output without loss on any increment. If labor *is* so supplied, it is contributing to the source of demands for complementary productive services, as well as for the inputs and outputs of non-competing activities generally, and whether or not investment in the labor in question turns out to be as profitable to entrepreneurs as they had expected. To put this proposition in a slightly different way, *potential* labor supply and the *potential* supply of complementary services do *not* contribute to the source of demands for non-competing things. It is only as *possible* inputs are valued or priced to become profitable (and hence *actual*) inputs that they are "supplied" and so express demands.

I anticipate the objection that if the quantities and values of "supplies" are identical in every case with the quantities and values of "demands", how can economists

79

talk of demands exceeding supplies and vice versa? It is simply a conventional but loose use of words. When the supply of a particular input or output increases, in the sense that the supply schedule moves forward and the demand schedule remains where it is, we traditionally describe the position which exists while the process of revaluing (repricing) is occurring (i.e., during the transition to a new equilibrium) by the phrase "supply exceeds demand," just as we say "the kettle boils" or the "candle is out" when we mean "the water boils" or "the flame is out." But at each moment of time, over a revaluation period, although the price per unit is falling, the conditions of "Walras' identity" are fulfilled, i.e., the amount and value of any thing "actually supplied" equals the amount and value "actually demanded."

In the real world, the process of revaluation proceeds in continuity. Entrepreneurs who offer increased supplies may at times be "groping," trying out the market, perhaps testing elasticities of demand for their product, gradually reducing the price demanded in order to discover the most profitable rate of production and/or of inventory clearance. They will often act in the expectation that potential customers will only gradually become aware of the availability of the product. Yet this does not imply that all "actual supplies" (values and quantities) will not always equal "actual demands" in both senses.

For instance, when inventories are accumulating unprofitably and the owners of the *unplanned* inventories, on gradually becoming aware of the unprofitability, are groping to discover the price (necessarily reduced in most cases) which will maximize prospective net receipts from their liquidation (so as to minimize any loss), we commonly say "supply exceeds demand," and we all understand what is meant. Similarly, when there is a "shortage" or rationing, we usually say that "demand exceeds supply," although what we really mean is that, at the price asked, more *would be* demanded if more were supplied. Hence I cannot conceive of any situation in which (using words in their everyday meaning) the value and amount demanded in any market fails to equal the value and amount supplied, even when inventories which are destined to have been unprofitably accumulated happen to be piling up, or when "shortages" or rationing occur. The price of a thing limits the amount of it which *can be* sold and hence the amount that *will be* purchased. A price imposed above the equilibrium between supply and demand will limit demand and a price imposed below the equilibrium will limit supply. In both cases, the disequilibrium means that the actual amounts supplied *and* demanded are less than they would have been in equilibrium.* And the same is true when normal inertias (lags in price adjustment) explain any disequilibrium. When an imposed price is below the equilibrium, and there are "shortages" (i.e., when many people who *would be* prepared to demand at the price asked if they could get the goods are prevented from demanding), the lucky individuals who do manage to demand obtain a value equal to the value of what is supplied. It might be useful to describe such values as "disequilibrium values." But the existence of the situation does not affect the significance of Say's law, which covers the case of non-price rationing as well as the kind of underpricing which exists when the right to purchase involves a special privilege, or the cost (inconvenience, discomfort, time spent) of standing in a queue, or good luck (the cost

---

*Clower appears to think that "traditional" analysis did not perceive the position. As he describes the situation, "perhaps the simplest way to define such measures is to suppose that actual transactions in any given market are always dominated by the 'short side' of the market; that is to say, market transactions are equal to planned market supply if demand is greater than supply, to planned market demand if supply is equal to or greater than demand".[1] What puzzles me in this passage is the word "suppose." Given downward sloping demand curves and upward sloping supply curves the 'short side' *must* always prevail. Clower refers to the situation as an "addendum to traditional theory."[2] Actually, I cannot remember any time since I read H. D. Henderson's *Supply and Demand* in the middle 1920's when I did not take it for granted.

81

being borne by the unlucky and by the community generally).

It is possible, then, for the withholding of supplies (and hence of demands) to be accompanied by non-price rationing (obvious or in various disguises), as under different kinds of repressed inflation (imposed price rigidities upwards intended to restrain inflationary pressures). Such withholdings have exactly the same contractionist consequences as other withholdings, unless dictated prices happen to be *selective*, imposed more or less in the manner in which free market pressures induce cost and price adjustments. In the latter case the "controls" *may* crudely restrain the effects of duress-imposed costs and in some measure countervail contractionist pressures.

Unemployment of labor in any case can not be said to be due, therefore, to *actual* labor supply exceeding demand. Nor is *wasteful* idleness of plant and equipment due to the supply of the services of such assets exceeding the demand for them, although more may have been provided than has turned out to be profitable. It is always possible for a greater original value to have been invested in certain assets than would have occurred if future demands for their services (or future prices of complementary services) had been accurately foreseen. But the value of "actually supplied" services of unwisely provided assets remains equal to the value of the services actually demanded. In the extreme case, supposed assets may be valueless: i.e., as we have seen (p. 35), unintended consumption equal to the whole value of the investment may have occurred. There is then neither any "actual demand" for, nor "actual supply" of, the services of the assets.

At times, Clower's and Leijonhufvud's point seems to be that (again for some reason arising out of the use of money) labor's offers to work at wage-rates which *would* have turned out to be profitable to entrepreneurs are, by reason of *unjustified* entrepreneurial pessi-

mism, refused by them (the pessimism being due to the absence of correct or recognized market signals—a defect in communications). But unjustified pessimism at any moment about prospective yields, however caused, tends merely to reduce the wage-rates or other input prices, the acceptance of which can *initiate* the process of restoring or maximizing the wages-flow and thereby (one would think) express the required signals unmistakably, generate justified entrepreneurial optimism and dissolve unjustified entrepreneurial pessimism.*
Hence if the situation described as "excess supply of labor" is viewed as I have suggested it should be, namely, as a condition of the economy under which some labor has been priced into unemployment (or into inferior work), although it would be demanded for its former employment if it were "actually supplied," then the reason for the unemployment is obvious—wage-rates maintained above the market-clearing levels; and in *this* case, the lower limits of market-clearing wage-rates are fixed by the next best employment activities open for each worker.

This brings me to the crucial point of my contribution. *Market-clearing wage-rates may conceivably be well below the levels at which the idle labor would be profitably utilizable if other workers generally were not simultaneously holding out for wage-rates higher than the immediate market-clearing levels.* *

I have been gradually forming the opinion of recent years that modern critics of Keynes and Keynesianism like Patinkin, Clower, Leijonhufvud and Yeager have been, without realizing it, approaching a perception that what they still call "effective demand" is nothing more than a view of demands in general *as they would come*

---

*In any case, I can conceive of no reasons why *the use of money* should give rise to pessimistic forecasting (See pp. 30-34).

*The reader should notice that this is another way of saying, "higher than is compatible with the maximization of labor's aggregate earnings at current prospective yields to investment."

to be if, in a condition of recession, and through the operation of Say's law, supplies were permitted to expand either by reason of downward cost and price adjustments or through unanticipated inflation (or not fully anticipated inflation). In other words, the notion of "aggregate effective demand" refers to the magnitudes of demands as they *could* be if supplies were released from withholding (i.e., if all inputs and outputs were priced consistently with the continuous, uninterrupted flow of all productive services through all the stages of production and into consumption).

In my book *Keynesianism,*[3] I referred to a passage from Lavington's *The Trade Cycle* (1922) in which it is obvious that Lavington saw things (in 1922) exactly as I do, and as *I think* Leijonhufvud, Clower and Yeager now do, in respect of what I have called "the hiatus." H. G. Browne's 1931 contribution, *Economic Science and the Common Welfare,* quoted at some length on this issue by Leland Yeager,[4] also contains a beautifully clear exposition of the point. "The inactivity of all," said Lavington, "is the cause of the inactivity of each. No entrepreneur can fully expand his output until others expand their output."[5] And this implies that the path to recovery, whether or not inflation is avoided, will be the determination of all input and all output prices in the light of existing, not ultimate, entrepreneurial prospects, i.e., when prices compatible with market-clearing requirements are determined. *

---

*In an appreciative critique, an anonymous reader, reporting to my publisher, comments on this issue:

"The theory of depression he has introduced is, in my opinion, original. He continuously maintains that it was the pre-Keynesian approach. Since I am not highly learned in the literature, I cannot say for certain this is untrue; but I can say I have never heard the theory before. Thus, although Hutt purports to be restating a traditional approach, it seems to me that he is introducing a new one."

But in writing this essay I felt myself that I was restating and perhaps clarifying what Cannan, Lavington, and H. G. Browne had clearly stated and other economists had accepted.

The whole issue in Clower's "dual-decision" hypothesis centers, then, on the relations between the *potential* profitability of production to satisfy what *would be* the workers' demands if the wage-rates for which they are holding out were appropriately lowered, and what entrepreneurs *would offer* for labor's inputs if they envisaged the profits which their acceptance of current terms *would yield*.

" . . . The other side of involuntary unemployment," says Clower, "would seem to be involuntary underconsumption," presumably meaning by the latter that *full* consumption *would be* that enjoyed in the absence of restraints on free-market pricing or unjustified entrepreneurial pessimism. He suggests that Keynes either had this hypothesis at the back of his mind, "or most of the *General Theory* is theoretical nonsense."[6] But he seems to think also that this theory is "damaging to orthodoxy" because "no trace of the (dual-decision) hypothesis is anywhere to be found" in the contemporary general equilibrium theory.[7] The fact is that the circumstances imagined were accepted as self-evident among the economists who tacitly recognized Say's law, whereas it was Keynes and his disciples who were somehow quite blind to it. *The General Theory* was indeed, as Clower says, "theoretical nonsense" for this very reason.

In 1922, Cannan never thought of commenting on Lavington's excellent exposition of the point, from which I have just quoted the crucial passage, when he reviewed the latter's book. That was, I think, because Cannan regarded the passage as nothing more than an excellent popularization of what every economist took for granted. I myself quoted that passage in 1963 because Keynes and the Keynesians seemed unaware of the relationship. Clower, who is now very laboriously breaking out of the chains of the Keynesian orthodoxy in which, I feel, he early became entangled, simply cannot believe that Keynes and his young advisers did not understand what he (Clower) now perceives.

It is possible that a mere semantic factor may have been responsible for some conceptual confusion here. This phrase "excess supply" of labor is simply a way of describing a *potential supply* which exceeds *current or actual supply* because pricing for its absorption into outputs (including direct consumption of services) has not yet occurred. Hence the word "excess" here could more appropriately be "deficient" or "insufficient"! An "excess" potential supply means a "deficient" actual supply. *More* will be "supplied," raising the source of demands for non-competing things, at wage-rates which raise prospective yields from investment in labor's inputs.

If inventories of outputs of any kind are accumulating (otherwise than for the planned "creation of 'time' or 'availability' utilities") it is one indication of "unduly high" prices causing or reflecting *withheld* "supplies" and hence *withheld* "demands" for other things. But any such unplanned stock-piling is a market signal to entrepreneurs to reduce the price and/or to transfer versatile resources (labor and assets) to the production of other things which have become *relatively* profitable. The *extent* of any required price reduction, in the actual world as well as in Walrasian theory, is in some measure a matter of "groping," "trial and error," "trying out," followed by changes in prices or in particular uses of resources. (p. 46 ff.)

But Leijonhufvud holds that in his situation of "unemployment disequilibrium," " . . . firms . . . are to some extent constrained by their inability to sell what they want at the prices of the moment."[8] My difficulty about this passage arises from the words "what they want." Under competition, I can imagine no constraints at all. Firms will be able to fix prices *calculated* to maximize yields; and they will be able to adjust "quantities"—rates of production and rates of sales—accordingly. "Prices of the moment" will, through the process referred to in the paragraph before, become such as clear the market either (a) through sales or (b) through completion of one or more stages in the production process (with or without sale to intermediaries).* [In case (b) the present discounted value of forecast ultimate sales will be the relevant price]. But any *new* curtailment of output imposed on a free market will have a depressive effect.

Turning now from supply to demand, we can say that labor is *demanded* for any activity when a *sufficient* wage-rate is offered to acquire whatever supply is actually forthcoming. In a co-ordinated economy, the term "sufficient" will have sole reference to *the net advantageousness of alternative employments* available to the workers whose services are sought.* But in all circumstances a wage-rate can be said to be "sufficient" when it is high enough to retain prospectively profitable workers in, or attract them into, that activity. We can, of course, following an inappropriate convention, say that the demand for labor in any occupation is "in excess" when more workers could be profitably employed in that occupation if they were available at ruling wage-rates. But then again the word "deficient" would be a better descriptive term. For it means that the wage-rate offered is *insufficient* to retain, or to attract (from other employments or from unemployment), all the labor which would be *potentially* profitably employable in that activity at the higher wage-rate. This is the clearest way of describing a situation in which there are frustrated incentives for *potential* supplies and *potential* demands to become *actual* supplies and *actual* demands. But every *actual* demand for labor always retains or attracts it. Otherwise it is not demanded!

*I.e., when investment in increased inventories for the production of "time utilities" is judged more productive than alternative uses of the capital involved.

*Individual workers will have different alternatives; but for simplicity I *assume* here that monopsonistic discrimination is ruled out. I have discussed this issue at length elsewhere. (*The Strike-Threat System*, Chapters 8, 9 and 12).

One final point. While market constraints on input prices through collusive agreements or duress-imposed values can be recognized as causing the most usual *initiating* withholdings of supplies, *induced* cumulative withholdings in non-competing fields *need* not occur mainly in those activities in which the most obvious abuses of monopolistic power are tolerated. Small firms confronted with unfavorable transfers of demand may not always be sufficiently competitive among one another to be forced to cut prices in emergent depression, although wise policy would exhort them to do so; while large firms, even when they possess some monopoly power, may well be in a position to read the signals more accurately. But it is at the cost or input stage that the more serious withholdings (initiatory or induced) are encountered.

1. R. W. Clower, *Monetary Theory*, p. 281.
2. *Ibid.*, p. 282.
3. Hutt, *Keynesianism*, p. 66.
4. Yeager, "The Keynesian Diversion", pp. 159-162.
5. F. Lavington, *The Trade Cycle*, London, P. S. King, 1922, p. 23.
6. Clower, *op. cit.*, p. 290.
7. *Ibid.*, p. 291.
8. Leijonhufvud, *On Keynesian Economics*, p. 57.

XII

PRICING FOR MARKET CLEARANCE

As I explained (on pages 41-42 and pages 82-86), if there is much unemployed labor, the reduction of wage-rates in any particular occupation needed to make "full employment" in it profitable will, in general, be a greater reduction than will be necessary if unemployed workers in other occupations generally are also concurrently trying to price their labor for its profitable employment. But even so, *ceteris paribus*, every downward wage-rate adjustment will not only tend to increase the profitability of employment in the occupation immediately affected but will contribute to a rise in the real value of wage outlets profitably offerable in non-competing fields.

To illustrate a thesis which does not quite accord with this analysis, Leijonhufvud uses a device of Walras'. He conceives of all prices being set every day to clear the market by an imaginary and infallible auctioneer, with entrepreneurs simply determining profitable quantities in the light of the prices so determined. We are asked to imagine for a certain day a possible labor supply which exceeds the actual supply (i.e., a condition of "excess supply") together with "excess demand for commodities" in the sense that, *if* the unemployed obtained employment, they would "devote their *entire* wage proceeds to consumption".[1] In such circumstances, Leijonhufvud says, the Walrasian auctioneer would have to raise the prices of consumers' commodities and reduce wage-rate offers.

Now to the extent to which certain wage-rates are "too high" in the sense of higher than the equilibrium value, it may mean (and *probably* does mean) that the *equilibrium* levels of other wage-rates are lower than they would otherwise be. But let us simply assume that the downward adjustments made increase the employment of labor (i.e., increase the workers' inputs supplied). In that case, they must enhance the flow of goods and services as a whole. Hence, the Walrasian auctioneer would have to raise the *relative* prices only of those goods of which the supplies did not increase by as much as the average, or for which demand increased by more than the average. Leijonhufvud imagines, however, the whole of the increased earnings being, as he puts it, "spent on consumption." Strictly speaking one "spends on consumption" only when one buys *services consumed as they are rendered.* "Consumption" is, as I have insisted (pp. 13-14), the *extermination* of power to demand, and hence, in itself, a depressive factor. What is *called* "spending on consumption" usually refers to replacement (partial or full) of a value equal to what has been consumed (of services or assets) whether the *inventories* replenished are in households or in warehouses, shops and factories. Hence Leijonhufvud means by "spent on consumption," I take it (in the terminology I myself prefer), "used for investment in replacement or to acquire services consumed as they are rendered." The replacement will probably be mainly of inventories of consumers' goods, i.e., goods of relatively short life. If so, it seems to me, his assumption implies that different portions of the stock of assets into which labor's services flow will increase *relatively* in value in proportion to the expected shortness of their lives, with services consumed directly increasing most in value, while long-life assets will tend to lose most in *relative* value.

However, Leijonhufvud holds that Walras' auctioneer would, as his first step in the "groping" process, reduce wage-rates as a means of restoring employment of labor and raise consumer goods prices in response to or in anticipation of the postulated increase in demand for such goods. But I do not see why Walras' auctioneer should raise the price of consumer goods unless his infallible forecast tells him that, with no time lag, labor's money income will be so increased by the reduction of wage-rates that, at unchanged consumer good prices, there would have to be some form of rationing. *

Here again, it seems that money is thought to be the root of all evil; for Leijonhufvud thinks that, *under conceptual barter*, through the "groping" process, there would be no difficulty and a co-ordinated economy would result. The Walrasian position is not simulated in a money economy, he says, because "there is no upward pressure on commodity prices" as fuller employment occurs and hence "no stimulus towards expanding production."[2] I do not understand this passage. For given Leijonhufvud's assumption that the newly employed workers devote all the *additional* income they produce (i.e., the whole value of their new contribution to inputs) to what he calls "consumption," the prices of services *consumed* or of short-life commodities *replaced* must be assumed to rise *relatively to the prices of long-life commodities.* In other words, if downward wage-rate adjustments *are* achieved, the consequence (under Leijonhufvud's assumption) will certainly be a rise in the prices of consumer goods *relative* to the prices of producer goods. On the assumption that monetary policy

---

*Moreover, if we make different assumptions, namely, that the newly employed workers produce only consumer goods, the auctioneer would *not* raise consumer goods prices because there would be increased supplies of such goods to meet the increased demands for them.

is *flexible*, that will mean an *absolute* rise in the prices of consumer goods as soon as the wages-flow begins to grow (i.e., as downward wage-rate adjustments are brought about) parallel with an absolute fall in the prices of producer goods. Of course, as we have seen, if monetary policy is rigid,* fuller employment must mean deflationary pressures because it means greater output, and *vice versa*. But I do *not* suggest that *this* is what Leijonhufvud has in mind.

In any case, it is *not* "upward pressures on commodity prices" *in general* which is the essential condition for expanding production. Prospective yields compatible with greater outputs may be established through those downward cost adjustments which enhance the wages and income flow. If the prices of a majority of inputs and outputs have been fixed too high for complete market clearance, whether through collusion, duress, or general entrepreneurial pricing errors, that is one way in which "supplies" (and hence "demands") can be withheld. But in practice, for political reasons, what may be called "the normal withdrawal of supplies" occurs, not through entrepreneurial pricing errors, but through *the forcing up of input prices relatively to output prices*, output prices still being, on the whole, consistent with market clearance of the reduced outputs that remain prospectively profitable. *

Nevertheless, Leijonhufvud suggests that (for some reason connected with the use of money) business forecasters will not see things as they are presumed to be in general equilibrium analysis. He says: "Not perceiving that more output is called for, individual firms will"

---

*I.e., if the "money supply" remains constant as the aggregate real value of money changes.

*Market-freeing action (like United States anti-trust) intended to deter one set of manufacturers or merchants from attempting to exploit the others (as producers or consumers) is seldom paralleled by action to restrain different groups of workers from trying to exploit their fellows, either as workers or in their consumer role.

turn down unemployed labor which offers itself at reduced wage-rates, *"even if no more than labor's marginal
product (evaluated at going prices) is being asked for."*
In other words, "prospective employers" who do not
perceive that "more output is called for" will not acquire
the additional labor "even if no more than the money wage
that the system would have in equilibrium is being asked
for."[3] The assumption here is that entrepreneurs expect
—but expect *wrongly*—that, in order to sell the additional output, they will have to reduce output prices by
an amount which would reduce prospective yields to the
point at which it would be unprofitable to employ the
cheapened labor which is offered.

It seems to me that, in the passage just quoted, Leijonhufvud conceives of "labor's marginal product" in a
different way from what I have always conceived of it.
I have always thought of marginal productivity in relation
to *prospective* yields. It would be better expressed as
"labor's marginal *prospective* product." But when
Leijonhufvud maintains that pessimistic entrepreneurs
will not give employment to workers who merely ask
their marginal product, *he appears to be thinking of
what their marginal product would eventually turn out to
be if workers generally were employed at market-
clearing wage-rates.* For at wage-rates equal to the
"marginal *prospective* product," all labor is immediately
employable; its actual employment will set in operation
the required "groping" process; this process will lead,
in subsequent periods, to a rise in labor scarcity; and
that scarcity will, in turn, result in entrepreneurs being
forced to offer real wage-rates which correspond to
labor's rising *realized* marginal product. Leijonhufvud
tacitly assumes that labor refuses to accept its present
marginal *prospective* product.

I should have said that "the equilibrium wage-rate"
at any moment is that which is established in the light
of whatever *prospective* yields happen to be at that
moment, *and however much the prospects are destined*

to change in the future. Admittedly, in the circumstances Leijonhufvud imagines, it might happen that, because entrepreneurs as a whole do not perceive the truth that a general reduction of duress-imposed labor costs magnifies the source of demands as a whole, they delay longer than is for their (and society's) advantage in accepting fallen wage-rate offers. But that only means that labor's marginal *prospective* product is further reduced, not that the wheels cannot be set spinning again by wage-rate adjustments, which is the topic under debate.

I suggest, then, that what Leijonhufvud is actually envisaging here is a situation which Say's law explains, namely, that the unemployed workers, although they have reduced their wage offer, have not reduced it sufficiently—in the light of unjustifiably pessimistic entrepreneurial expectations—to release their full potential contribution to supplies and hence to the source of demands. But when wage offers *have* been sufficiently adjusted for entrepreneurs generally to accept them, each output expansion is contributing to a state of affairs in which, through dynamic reactions set going, higher marginal prospective labor products *will* generally emerge and higher money wage-rates will be forced by the market. Entrepreneurs are indeed engaged in the Walrasian "groping" process; and if the workers *did* price their services initially in consistency with whatever entrepreneurial forecasts happened to be, entrepreneurs would soon find themselves confronted with the harsh realities of labor shortage.

Hence Leijonhufvud's contention that "there is no stimulus towards expanding production"[4] when unemployed workers offer their services (because the prices of end products do not rise) does not hold if "*the offer*" of the workers' services means "the actual supply"— the actual sale of —those services. The employment of formerly unemployed workers *is* in itself an expansion of the source of demands; and if we find the concept of "stimulus" useful, we can say that every particular increase in employment of labor "stimulates" an expansion of non-competing outputs in the sense of tending to raise (a) the prospective values of such outputs and hence (b) the real wage-rates it is profitable to offer for labor to produce them.

But, says Leijonhufvud, "once the multiplier has done its dirty work, the system may remain in an unemployment state although the money wage is 'right' from the standpoint of over-all equilibrium."[5] If he had said "*ultimate* equilibrium" instead of "over-all equilibrium" here, I could have accepted it, although I should think of the cumulative decline in activity implied by Say's law as "the multiplier." As it is, the wage-rate Leijonhufvud envisages is "wrong" from the standpoint of *present* equilibrium. He maintains, however, that in "unemployment disequilibrium" producers will not be willing to absorb the excess "supply of labor . . . at a wage corresponding to the real wage that would satisfy the Walrasian problem".[6] But this problem is solved only when "ultimate equilibrium" has been reached, while he ignores *the path to* that equilibrium. As long as the workers generally hold out for the higher remuneration which the market would be destined eventually to force if they did not hold out, they will never move towards it.

Leijonhufvud (like Clower) regards the situation as a "communication failure." He says: "The unemployed supply labor and demand bread. . . . But . . . the demand is an 'ineffective' demand that does not constitute a stimulus to increased (and labor-demanding) production of bread. The *market signals* presupposed in general equilibrium analysis *are not transmitted*."[7] But is it not rather the reverse—a case of market signals being ignored or misinterpreted? The workers are *not* demanding bread until they pay for it the price which is being asked; and they are *not* supplying labor until they accept wage-rates that appear profitable to entrepreneurs. And if a general failure to pay the price asked for bread is not a transmitted signal that *present* prices (not the *ultimate* prices) of grain, milling, baking and retailing are somehow wrong, I do not know what could be; while the layoff or unemployment of workers is surely equally a market signal that *present* wage-rates (not *ultimate* wage-rates) are "unduly high."

At times, Leijonhufvud seems to be using the term "demand" to mean what I should call "desire" and the term "effective demand" to mean what I call "demand" as distinct from "desire." When he says that unemployed workers "supply" labor and "demand" bread, but they do not demand bread "effectively," he means that entrepreneurs are unjustifiably pessimistic and do not accept the offer of labor at its reserve price, *which price means the withholding of its supply*, so that although the workers would *like* to buy bread, they have nothing to offer for it and hence cannot demand it.

What *is* conceivable, however, is that earnings of formerly unemployed labor (other than bakers), and increased earnings of bakers *could* mutually justify one another *if they* came about *spontaneously and simultaneously*. That this may not happen because the true situation is not perceived is exactly the point that Cannan was making in 1933 (*see* pp. 57-59). Leijonhufvud is wrong, however, if he implies that pricing adjustments are incapable of bringing about the recovery sought. The exploratory initial wage-rate cuts I have envisaged are the required mechanism—the first step in Walrasian "groping."*

The problem of rapid and accurate transmission of market signals is tied up with the separate problem of

---

*Actually, a failure of communications, the absence of prompt signals to changing conditions or the absence of prompt response to such signals, or wrong interpretation of them is no explanation of the *idleness* of men or assets. *It is an explanation of waste* (that is, non-optimal *use* of men and assets) because it means tardy adjustments to change instead of expeditious adjustments, that is all. In other words, it does not explain *non-use* of valuable (i.e. potentially demanded) services. It explains *wrong-use*. (*See* pp. 104-109).

the inferences through the medium of which all decision-makers must extrapolate from past events. But if policy aimed throughout at the improvement of price flexibility, entrepreneurs would surely learn that any inadvertently caused slowing down of economic activity would be early reversed through market-selected cost and price adjustments.

These considerations are relevant to Leijonhufvud's discussion of the response of the economy to "changes in saving behavior," to which I have already referred. He brings in here, as I have said, what I regard as a wholly separate factor, liquidity-preference. (See Chapter X.) But he holds that "producers' demand forecasts do not respond in an appropriate and reliable fashion" to such changes;[8] and he explains later that if "entrepreneurial expectations were to approximate more closely to the demand that would actually be experienced . . . , they would become self-fulfilling. . . . "[9] Admittedly, the net accumulation of assets which the achievement of savings implies[10] should, if perceived, enhance profit prospects;* while the optimism of one entrepreneur will justify the optimism of another (in a non-competing field). But this does not detract from the importance of the principle that the *path* to the creation of *justified* entrepreneurial expectations is wage-rates (and other prices constituting costs) which are sensitively adjusted to entrepreneurial forecasts, *however unjustifiably pessimistic those forecasts may happen to be at the outset.* On the next page, Leijonhufvud explains: "Entrepreneurial demand forecasts are attuned to a continuation of depression. The immediate objective is to change them while meddling as little as possible with interest rates that are already at (or below) the level

*Because (*ceteris paribus*) if the aggregate real value of assets increases, then irrespective of the composition of the stock, it means that the prospective income stream from them (which, discounted, represents their capital value) is also enhanced, as well as the yield to labor's efforts which will increase absolutely and, *ceteris paribus*, relatively.

97

they would have been in equilibrium. Direct government expenditure would do the trick."[11]

Because *ultimate* equilibrium is destined to be achieved at higher wage-rates than appear profitable under entrepreneurial pessimism, it *is* theoretically possible that an increase in MV* ("increased expenditure," irrespective of whether it is directed to public works) would not mean any departure from a policy of "monetary flexibility," i.e., it *might* not have any inflationary consequences. (The rate of interest would not have to fall below the "natural" level.) The wage-rates for which the workers were holding out would justify themselves (through Say's law repercussions) by proving to be profitable after all, and the workers' initiatives (to reduce labor costs) could be avoided. But if that *is* what is intended, it is a criticism of the monetary authority which, it is *assumed*, fails to recognize the very high elasticity of labor supply that is implied. Purposeless monetary stringency is tacitly alleged therefore—perhaps what Leijonhufvud envisages as "perverse" action by a central bank or treasury.

The passage I am discussing is, however, capable of a different interpretation, namely, that the officials who decide on "direct government expenditure" are tacitly assumed to be shrewder judges of prospective yields than business entrepreneurs. *On that assumption,* during depression the provision of such public works as taxpayers are predicted to demand as recovery occurs —not boondoggling—is justified. If the labor required is then recognized as temporarily cheap, the public incentive to invest in it (and so contribute to the source of demands) will be enhanced. But the question remains: Why should not shrewd businessmen perceive the profit to be won from temporarily cheap labor at least as wisely as government officials?

My own diagnosis of the origins of entrepreneurial forecasts "attuned to a continuation of depression" dif-

*I.e., an increase in "money supply" or an increase in its "activation."

fers from Leijonhufvud's. During this century at least, that pessimism has been, I judge, far more often justified than unjustified. Thus, in the situation to be described on pp. 135-7, entrepreneurs confronted with the depression were reacting realistically to a situation in which (i) the toleration of private duress or collusion to bring about "wage-push," or to maintain certain prices, and (ii) so-called "unemployment insurance" and other government action tending to render certain wage-rates or prices rigid, were frustrating rapid co-ordinative adjustments and exterminating prospective yields to investments, especially in such improvements of, or additions to, fixed capital as were subject to prospective strike-threat pressures. As a whole, entrepreneurs may not have clearly perceived the causes of the situation. But their apparent timidity in so-called slump periods was always, I suggest, a consequence of the price mechanism having been prevented from fulfilling its co-ordinative role. With the onset of recession, *sheer realism* prompted a reluctant perception that, to avoid individual disaster, the distasteful step of laying-off labor and working fixed assets at below technical capacity was quite unavoidable; and in the depth of depression a similar *well-founded* interpretation of the situation obstructed recovery.

One reason for my judgment that entrepreneurial pessimism in the circumstances of this century's depressions has been due to effective market signals correctly interpreted, rather than the reverse, is that forecasting acumen and risk-taking propensities cannot be assumed to be evenly shared within any industry. If labor costs are no longer unprofitably high, i.e., if the wage-rates for which the workers are holding out have been reduced (because bidding for the labor trained for, or attached to, an industry has been weak) those entrepreneurs who are more enterprising or better forecasters than the rest will be able to profit by getting in first. The shrewder or bolder will thereby steal a march on the others, in spite of the immediate demand for the product of the industry being well below what it is destined to be. They will profitably provide the additional outputs which the more timid or less perspicacious were wrongly afraid would lead to losses. The greater the extent to which unjustified pessimism causes some entrepreneurs to hold back, the greater will be the special yields to be won by those who do not; and the success of the latter will emit market signals to activate the others. Such considerations reinforce my judgment that in practice the entrepreneurial gloom which is typical of depression reflects wise insight, even when some concessions in respect of wage-rates have been made.

I conclude that Leijonhufvud has not, as he thinks, shown that "unemployment may persist even with the 'right' level" of money wage-rates, unless *he* means by "the right level" (in any employment) what *I* call "the wrong level" because it is not adjusted to *current* entrepreneurial assessments of profitability, right or wrong, and although the *ultimate* level may be destined to be much higher. In so far as any recession, having once begun, has become self-perpetuating or self-aggravating, that has not been due to successive cost and price reductions. It has been due to the opposite—(a) resistances to co-ordinative cost and price reductions and (b) entrepreneurial recognition of the unwillingness of governments to perform their "classical" task.

Everything I have said about the depressive effects on the economy of pricing labor's inputs above their market-clearing values in any given state of prospective yields applies equally, of course, to the pricing of the services of complementary factors. Not only the contractual claimants, but the residual claimants on the value of outputs may be in a position to contrive scarcities, thereby reducing their contribution to the source of demands for non-competing inputs and outputs. No less than labor employing the strike-threat, the

100

owners of industrial assets in any field may gain at the expense of the prosperity of the community as a whole. Thus far I have stressed the responsibility of "unduly-high" wage-rates (in relation to prospective yields) for the slowing down of economic activity, partly because Clower and Leijonhufvud seem to regard labor costs· as the crucial factor and partly because, on empirical grounds,* I share that apparent judgment. Statistical enquiries into income distribution have established the fact that, in general, it is the owners of assets whose relative incomes contract most in depression. Moreover, students of business administration have noticed how, during the onset of depression, managements do everything in their power to avoid the necessity of lay-offs; and, as the situation worsens and physical assets begin to operate at below full technical capacity, with consequential declining residues, they (the managers) become scared of their own displacement which, in the case of elderly executives or those of middle age could, in some instances, mean disaster for them. Typically, they are almost desperately anxious to get the wheels turning again.

I am not suggesting that collusion among managements trying "not to spoil the market," as market-clearing prices tend to fall in any industry, may not exert a depressive influence on demands for the inputs and outputs of non-competing industries. Nor do I ignore the possibility that prices charged by natural monopolies may not be incompetently controlled, whether as a result of lobby pressures or otherwise. I certainly believe that anti-trust or its equivalent (if it could be rescued from vote-gathering influences and *its purpose explicitly recognized and declared)** would be a rational method

---

*For reasons discussed at length in my recently published *The Strike-Threat System.*[12]

*Its purpose being that of maximizing aggregate profits, i.e., the raising of prospective yields in general, so as to cause increased competition for labor and the maximization of the absolute wages-flow.

101

of contributing to that objective and the full employment it implies. But recognition of this in no way weakens the significance of Say's law. It is yet another possibility that illustrates the all-pervasiveness of that law.

I have mentioned that both Leijonhufvud and Clower place very great stress on the imperfections of the information or communication process as a cause of the *hiatus*. But the kind of communication or information required for the coordination of the economy takes the form of market pressures;* and these pressures are exerted through loss-avoidance, profit-seeking incentives. Faced with such market signals as shrinking or accumulating inventories, entrepreneurs react by changing the rates of liquidation of different inventories *via* the price changes which they forecast will effect the desired results.

---

*It is important to recognize that other types of communication of information are *technical* in nature, irrelevant to the problems we are here discussing.

1. Leijonhufvud, *Keynes and the Classics*, p. 34.
2. *Ibid.*, p. 35.
3. *Ibid.*, p. 35.
4. *Ibid.*, p. 35.
5. *Ibid.*, pp. 35-6.
6. Leijonhufvud, *On Keynes and Keynesian Economics*, p. 90.
7. Leijonhufvud, *Keynes and the Classics*, p. 36.
8. *Ibid.*, p. 38.
9. *Ibid.*, p. 40.
10. See Hutt, *Keynesianism*, Ch. XI.
11. Leijonhufvud, *Keynes and the Classics*, p. 41.
12. W. H. Hutt, *The Strike-Threat System*, N.Y., Arlington House, 1973.

XIII

SUB-OPTIMAL EMPLOYMENT
AND CHRONIC
UNEMPLOYMENT

Only when inputs are widely priced incompatibly with current prospective yields, and output prices are widely fixed incompatibly with current money income and consumer price expectations do we find reasons for a *general* contraction in economic activity leading to chronic under-utilization or "sub-optimal utilization" of productive capacity. Cumulative, self-aggravating failures to maintain activity are due to pricing defects which first dam up the source of demands and then prevent the dam from being breached. In other words, the condition which Leijonhufvud and Clower seem to believe Keynes (to his credit) somehow perceived but failed to enunciate (while other economists had not even perceived it) emerges when (irrespective of rectifiable entrepreneurial error) "wage push" is allowed to occur or any other form of pricing which relies on the overruling of free market pressures. If our empirical studies tell us that "wage-push" *is* the initiating cause, the repercussions are *firstly*, initiatory layoffs of labor and wasteful idleness of assets (possibly including wastefully held inventories) in the firm or industry in which labor costs are raised; and *secondly*, induced layoffs and wasteful idleness *in non-competing* sectors, due to wage-rate rigidities, price rigidities, and sectionalist barriers generally in

103

those sectors.* Each such contraction tends, in turn, to induce similar contractions in yet other sectors.

But what could still be merely temporary idleness, merging into full but "sub-optimal" (wasteful, *relatively* unremunerative and unproductive) employment tends, as we have seen, to become *chronic idleness* through subsidies financed by *income transfers.* Subsidized non-use of valuable resources (through *some* forms of unemployment compensation, relief handouts, price supports, and so forth) prevents or discourages displaced men and assets from finding alternative, "sub-optimal" employments which could otherwise *mitigate* the extent to which the source of demands is repressed and recession aggravated, as well as preventing or discouraging such idle resources from returning to formerly profitable activities and supplying inputs at costs compatible with prospective yields to investment.

The difficulty economists trained in the Keynesian tradition have in recognizing the nature of the failure to clear the labor market, and the real causes of the phenomenon of chronic unemployment of labor, stands as a powerful hindrance to clarity of thought in their expositions. For instance, H. I. Grossman believes that Keynes accepted and enunciated "classical" theory in respect of the "unemployment" of labor.[1] Certainly Keynes himself *thought* (in 1936) that he was accepting the then current theory. In the words of *The General Theory,* "the real wage earned by a unit of labor has a unique inverse correlation with the volume of employment". Well, duress-raised labor costs do reduce the profitability of employment *in any occupation.* Yet Grossman objects (citing statistical enquiries of Kuh and Bodkin) that "despite repeated attempts, such a pattern of real wages has not been observed."[2] He is, however, thinking of the aggregate wages-flow, not of the price of labor in any industry or firm.

Now all these economists, including Keynes, *confuse the pricing of some resources out of supply—the process of withholding some resources from their existing occu-*

---

*Such as labor union "demarcations," apprenticeship restraints, occupational licensing, minimum wage enactments, etc.

pations—with something quite different, namely, the failure of the displaced resources to accept "sub-optimal employments"—the next best employments available. And this is a matter of (a) *the alternative outlets* (the versatility of men and assets laid off) and (b) *the incentives* to accept those alternatives. I mentioned before the most important *disincentives,* in referring to subsidized idleness—"unemployment compensation," relief handouts, price supports, etc.,[*] disincentives which equally operate to obstruct the labor-cost adjustments essential for recovery of the wages-flow. The truth is that, during the present century, employable people have been increasingly able in the western world, through income transfers (including private transfers—"charity"), to survive without contributing through work to the source of demands, and without an income from their own savings or inherited property. In the United States at present, persons in this class can live in what the overwhelming majority of mankind would regard as affluence. But even in the very low income countries there are a host of other factors which may cause large numbers of people of conventional working age to refuse such contractually remunerated employment as is available, and to survive (however miserably) without a contractual income from work.

Hence there are no reasons for expecting the arbitrary magnitudes which are termed "unemployment" in different countries to be closely correlated with the rate of layoffs. This reality appears to me almost to make nonsense of some statistical correlations between average wage-rates and "unemployment," however the latter is defined.

Chronic "unemployment" of labor (such as existed in the 1930s) is certainly not due to any inability of the

[*]The fact that such mitigations may seem to be patently just in a society that permits and encourages· poverty creation and the aggravation of inequalities of opportunity and income (e.g., through tolerance of the strike-threat system; apprenticeship restraints; occupational licensing; minimum wage-rates; demoralization through relief; and restraints on the accumulation of wage-multiplying assets *via* taxation levied for vote-purchasing objectives) does not affect the reality that the subsidization of idleness exacerbates social injustices.

pricing mechanism, freed from the barriers of strike-threat duress and politically determined minima, to clear the labor market. The wages-flow can always be restored, when "unemployment" of any kind has developed, by pricing labor's inputs compatibly with prospective yields, which means within reach of unin-flated income and consistently with price expectations. And market-selected wage-rate and price adjustments can achieve this result not only by releasing for more productive, higher-paid work, those workers who have been forced into "sub-optimal employment," but by restoring "employment" in the sense of absorbing workers who have been in subsidized idleness or actively prospecting for the most favorable employment outlets.* This is the true "classical" understanding of the relation between the cost of labor's inputs and the profita-bility of investing in those inputs;* and no statistical studies have disclosed any facts that might in the least disturb it.

Leland Yeager is one of the few contemporary econ-omists to refer explicitly to the relevance of what I have called (for men and assets) "sub-optimal employ-ment"—in Yeager's words, the fact that "misallocation wastes can persist without idleness waste."[3] But he believes, if I understand him correctly, that the inferior employments available to workers laid-off through

---

*This discussion of the "unemployment" condition is unduly simplified. My book *The Theory of Idle Resources* (1939) is entirely devoted to an analysis of the different reasons why valuable services of men and assets are, at times, not purchased. For instance, a laid-off worker may be refusing contractual employment offers because he is prospecting for better outlets, which he can sometimes do most efficiently if he is not *contractually* engaged. As with all prospecting, such (basically entrepreneurial) efforts are really *remunerated employment, but with the remuneration being received later,* through the superior employment that is the reward of a wise or lucky search for a job. The "prospecting" may be subsidized out of income transfers or financed out of the individual's own capital (e.g., from actuarially sound unemployment insurance).

*I maintained, in *The Theory of Idle Resources,* that my contribution was "pure orthodoxy." I regarded that work as original only in the sense that it tried to make more clear what pre-Keynesian ("classical") economists really envisaged when they thought of "unemployment."

duress-imposed costs, and for assets displaced thereby, are unimportant mitigations because demand will be "deficient" for the inputs in alternative employments.[4] Certainly the cumulative effects of collusive or governmental cost-raising and price-raising operate to reduce still further the contractual remuneration at which the victims among the workers can alleviate the detriment imposed upon them, and also to reduce still further the residual yields of owners of displaced assets (which may have some versatility). This does not imply, however, that the condition is *unimportant.*

In my judgment, the mitigation can be substantial; although I certainly do not regard "sub-optimal full employment" as a tolerable condition. Chronic unemployment is conspicuous. Chronic misallocations are sometimes hardly recognizable and, in their most burdensome manifestations, often wholly unrecognizable. *Yet the wastes implied under "sub-optimal employment" are, as I see things, normally the most virulent form which wastes can take, both in prolonged depression and in inflation-maintained "prosperity."* When duress-imposed costs are allowed to repress the source of demands for decades (as I judge has happened in Britain since World War II), *the composition of the whole stock of assets becomes adversely affected, just as does the composition of "the stock of skills" acquired and the particular occupations to which workers "become attached."*

Grossman's theory of unemployment differs from Keynes' in that whereas the latter relied upon the reduction of real wage-rates for recovery, the former holds that the recovery of "aggregate demand" (the restoration of the source of demands) is possible (*via* inflation) "even with the real wage-rate unchanged," so that, under deficient aggregate demand, "the level of employment is unaffected by changes in real wages."[5] Grossman's presentation illustrates excellently how seriously astray some Keynesian-trained economists have been led and how poorly they have understood "classical economics." *Of course* the restoration of employment is compatible "with *the* real wage-rate unchanged," in the sense of the average wage-rate, *provided unem-*

*ployed workers are reckoned in the averages as having
a wage-rate of nil.* Indeed, recovery is not only *compatible with* a considerable *rise* in "the real wage-
rate" in this sense *but may be expected to bring it
about.* This applies whether the recovery is achieved
by deceiving the community about the planned speed and
duration of inflation or, much less unjustly and more
potently, through the initial market-selected wage-rate
and price adjustments needed for the gradual restoration of the wages-flow. Either policy can raise the
average *real* wage-rate while, under the assumption of
monetary flexibility, downward wage-rate adjustments will raise the average *money* wage-rate also.
This result may be expected (i) because, through reducing costs in relation to prospective prices in
activities where unprofitable cost-price ratios have
previously ruled, workers whose wage earnings have
for some time been zero (including some in subsidized
idleness) will begin to receive positive wage incomes;
(ii) because workers laid off into "sub-optimal" employments may be expected to return to more valuable
work; and (iii) (most important) because, through the
dynamic repercussions of Say's law, demands for outputs
and hence for labor, will be rising in real terms in all
non-competing sectors.

It remains necessary to deal briefly with Keynes'
objection (a fallacy which has not yet been eradicated)
that the workers cannot effectively cut their real wage-
rates directly, so as to make larger outputs profitable,
because that will in turn induce price cuts and thereby
prevent any reduction of the average *real* wage-rate.
There is no reason whatsoever why, in depression,
widely adopted wage-rate cuts *should* bring about
general cuts in the prices of output; for *firstly,* all
labor absorbed will be augmenting the source of demands,
and *secondly,* only under a deflationary monetary
policy (perhaps due to monetary rigidity) will initial
cuts in wage-rates fixed above full employment values
cause a defensibly weighted price index to fall. Hence,
under flexible monetary policy, the reduction of such
wage-rates as have been forced above the level that
clears the market for labor (which will occur in each

case as a reduction of *money* wage-rates) must, *ceteris paribus*, raise the average money wage-rate also, just as rapidly as outputs in general recover.

The policy implications of the "classical" theory which Keynes attacked (in relation to recovery from depression) can be summarized as follows. *The implicit aim was to achieve a higher wages-flow and hence a higher average real wage-rate* together with an increased flow of real income generally. But that process does require *initial* adjustments that bring down the costs of inputs to values which are related to prospective yields to investment in those inputs *in the existing state of depression.* The acceptance of these values will *always* mitigate the harsh consequences of non-market impositions on the co-ordinating price mechanism; but as I have insisted, *while these values may be well below those which are destined to rule as prospective yields recover, initial acquiescence in them may be inescapable for non-inflationary recovery from depression.*

To recapitulate, it is through restraints on the co-ordinative process that the source of demands can come to be cumulatively constrained. This is the origin of the condition that macro-economists so inappropriately call "increasingly deficient aggregate effective demand." Through such constraints, employment outlets remain available only at continuously falling real remuneration. The process can be reversed by unemployed (or sub-optimally employed) persons accepting jobs at labor costs which are related to *current* prospects of yields.

1. H. I. Grossman, "Was Keynes a Keynesian?", *Journal of Economic Literature*, 1972.
2. *Ibid.*, p. 28.
3. L. Yeager, "The Keynesian Diversion," p. 155.
4. *Ibid.*, pp. 154-155.
5. Grossman, *op. cit.*, p. 29.

XIV

HARRY G. JOHNSON'S VIEW
OF PRE-KEYNESIAN
ORTHODOXY

We are now in a position to consider
Harry G. Johnson's judgment (as dis-
closed in his 1970 Richard Ely Lecture[1]) of the economists
whose teachings Keynes is generally believed to have
"debunked". The most important attribute of what
Johnson calls "the prevailing orthodoxy" or "the established orthodoxy" of the 1920s and 1930s was its tacit
reliance upon Say's law. Johnson does not specifically
refer to the supposed deficiencies of this law *and now
quite possibly accepts it*; he does not defend the original
Keynesian teachings that seemed to challenge it; and
his diagnosis of the reasons for the infectious spread
of Keynesian ideas (reasons wholly unconnected with the
scientific merit of those ideas) is incomparably the
most convincing that has yet appeared.* Nevertheless he
charges that, in the 1930s, there existed " . . . an established orthodoxy which (was) clearly inconsistent with
the most salient facts of reality . . . its principles and
slogans. . . . (were) . . . demonstrably in conflict with
the facts of every day experience . . . the prevailing
orthodoxy could neither explain nor cope with" the situa-

---

*Apart from my own![2]

tion which had been created.[3] The pre-Keynesians were "hypnotized by the notion that money is merely a veil cast over real phenomena . . . and attempted to explain what were essentially monetary phenomena by real causes."[4]* And Johnson accepts Patinkin's charge that the prevailing school of the 1930s assumed "a tendency to automatic full employment."[5] Hence the "obvious irrelevance of orthodox economics to real problems"[6] at that time opened the way for a new theory. But have I not shown how Say's law explains the periodic emergence of an automatic tendency to unemployment as long as governments are allowed to act (as they typically do, of course) for the private benefit of vote-controlling interests, and neglect their "classical" function of preventing the depressive consequences of scarcity contrivance through private coercion or collusion?

In 1961, Johnson wrote that Keynes had been "polemically right"[7] in the shock tactics he employed in 1936, because it had become essential to destroy respect for the "orthodox" tradition which simply did not have the right or acceptable answers. Such answers as it offered were not "sensible,"[8] whereas *The General Theory* rationalized a sensible policy that had hitherto been resisted on purely dogmatic grounds."[9]

Johnson's attitude is clarified in his 1970 lecture. "New ideas," he says, "win a public and professional hearing, not on their scientific merits, but on whether or not they promise a solution to important problems that the established orthodoxy has proved itself incapable of solving."[10] He intends this truth to apply (I believe) both to the established "classical orthodoxy" of the 1920s and 1930s as well as to the established Keynesian orthodoxy of today. But *there is a radical difference between the two "orthodoxies." When Keynesian ideas were revolutionary, they were tailor-made for political acceptability. The "classical" ideas that Keynes tried to ridicule would have demanded outstanding statesmanship for their*

---

*Johnson's assertion would have been acceptable if he had written "pricing causes" instead of "real causes."

electoral acceptance, and there was no outstanding British statesman in the mid-thirties who had really grasped the issues.

A possible interpretation of Johnson's contention (and I guess that it is at any rate *partly* what is in his mind —although he does not say so) is that the economists of the 1920s and 1930s who adhered to "the prevailing orthodoxy" were failing to communicate—failing to persuade governments to apply classical constraints (and hence failing to inspire the policies needed to bring about non-inflationary full employment and prosperity). "Orthodox" theories were incapable of solving the problems of the day, not through their "scientific" demerits, but because it was absurd to expect governments to accept them. If this *is* the charge it has some substance; but we must not forget that governments were being assured all the time, by Keynesian academicians, that there *was* an easier way out than remedies which would antagonize a pressure group of dominating political influence.

Now it occurs to me that, assuming this interpretation of Johnson's position does not misrepresent it, quite possibly he himself *is* "polemically right" today in disparaging economists who failed to recommend politically acceptable remedies. If his insistence that "classical" economics was "wrong" in the 1930s means (a) that economists did not effectively press for the policies required for the restoration of prosperity; or (b) that through poor exposition of "classical" economics, opinion-makers and governments did not understand what the economists were saying; or (c) that governments dared not formulate policies in the light of "classical" principles if they wished to retain office; or (d) that governments procrastinated in the hope that there might be a less painful way out (as Keynes and his supporters seemed to be promising), then Johnson can contend that now, in the 1970s, "classical" economics is right *because circumstances are such that governments may at last be forced to listen to its message.* Just as the "established

HARRY G. JOHNSON'S VIEW

orthodoxy" of the 1930s was, through political unaccepta-
bility, "inconsistent with the most salient facts of reality"
of that period, so in the 1970s Keynesian economics suf-
fers (Johnson's words) from an "inability to prescribe for
what has come to be considered the major social problem
—inflation. . . ."[11] The times are therefore propitious
for the abandonment of the dominant economic theories
and policies of the last three decades.

When governments are becoming increasingly dis-
traught, owing to a growing recognition that only *accelerating* inflation or totalitarian-type price and
wage controls can prevent unemployment (through
planned inflation at last coming to be almost universally
expected), when they perceive (as they are at least
beginning to suspect) that they have "a tiger by the
tail,"* they may be in a mood to learn that unless they
apply "the classical medicine," they are heading for
disaster. Hence, for the purposes of press, political
platform and pulpit, we may perhaps fruitfully try a
tactical (although false) admission that, *in the 1930s,
"classical" economics was wrong on essentials. But
things have now changed. Today the old, discarded
teachings are right!* In other words, it is conceivable
that any case for returning to sound economic doctrine
must, to be plausible, and hence to be effective, pander
to long inculcated stereotypes about "classical" economics
having plunged the western economic world into cata-
strophic depression, despite the reality being diametrically opposite. I am not sure that this *is* partly Johnson's
position, although I think it is a tenable position.

In fact, however, the truths of "classical" economics,
as I interpret them, are universal. They hold and are
equally relevant for the understanding of all historical
periods and under all economic frameworks and, *where
opinion-makers have grasped the message*, equally
relevant for policy. And they will be no less true when

*Hayek's phrase. See A Tiger by the Tail, a symposium of Hayek's writings
on Keynesianism, edited by Sudha Shenoy, I.E.A., 1972.

113

today's economists have disguised and obscured them by clothing them in the modern jargon and setting them to mathematics.

But suppose I have here misinterpreted the reasons for Johnson's judgment that pre-Keynesian "orthodox" economics was not "sensible" and could neither cope with nor explain the situation which preceded the "Keynesian revolution." Suppose he means that charge to be taken literally. In that case, I ask the reader to consider the question: exactly what teachings of the "prevailing orthodoxy" or the "established orthodoxy" are considered not to have been "sensible"? When I myself try to think of the most apposite description of the approach of *the majority* of the non-Keynesian economists of the 1920s and 1930s it is just that word "sensible" which first occurs to me.

I should say that the chief attributes of the pre-Keynesian "classical" approach to economics were (i) a realistic recognition of the dynamic character of the economic process—*clearer in the Austrian tradition than in the Marshallian*—and in particular an awareness of the importance of the continuous revision of entrepreneurial expectations in response to continuous changes in the data ("market signals" as we term them today); (ii) a realistic recognition of the sluggishness with which, in certain sectors of the economy, values in exchange (prices) asked or offered, particularly in the case of labor, were adjusted to changing circumstances*; (iii) a realistic awareness of the irrationalities which were influencing the valuing and pricing function, and particularly what we today call "the money illusion"*; (iv) an intuitive perception that Say's law explained the phenomena which resulted from sluggishness in ad-

---

*In the current political and institutional setup.

*The subjective valuation of the money unit and money's worth on people's scales of preference in a manner which is not correlated with the purchasing power (real value) of the unit.

justment to change, such as boom, depression, and *cycles of idleness* in men and assets. *

Now as we have seen, it is in respect of the relations between monetary (including fiscal) policy and economic policy as a whole that the alleged inadequacies of the "prevailing orthodoxy" are most often assumed to lie, and in the next chapter I shall first direct attention to the teachings of the 1930s on that branch of the subject. Just what were the relevant blind spots of the non-Keynesians here? How far did they in fact try "to explain what were essentially monetary phenomena by real causes"?

*Idleness which occurred in spite of the fact that services of idle men and assets were valuable, i.e., *capable* of being demanded.

1. H. G. Johnson, *The Keynesian Revolution and the Monetarist Counter-Revolution*, A.E.R., May, 1971.
2. "Reflections on the Keynesian Episode," in *Toward Freedom*, Ed. F. A. Harper, 1971.
3. Johnson, A.E.R., 1971, *op. cit.*, p. 3.
4. *Ibid.*, p. 4.
5. *Ibid.*, p. 11.
6. *Ibid.*, p. 4.
7. H. G. Johnson, *The General Theory after 25 Years*, A.E.R., P & P, May 1961, p. 26.
8. *Ibid.*, p. 26.
9. Johnson, A.E.R., 1971, *op. cit.*, p. 12.
10. *Ibid.*, p. 12.
11. *Ibid.*, p. 7.

XV

THE POSITION OF "THE PREVAILING ORTHODOXY" OF THE 1920s AND 1930s

A difficulty we meet in considering H. G. Johnson's views on the issue raised in Chapter I is that of *identifying* "the prevailing orthodoxy," unless the common, but usually tacit, acceptance of Say's law is supposed to define the group disparaged. That this may perhaps be meant is suggested by Johnson's allegations that "a tendency to automatic full employment" was assumed and that money was thought of as a mere "veil." But when (in 1932) Cannan blamed "the reigning school of monetary experts" for the economic troubles of that time (in his Presidential address to the Royal Economic Society), he was obviously not thinking of money as a "mere veil." Nor were the "monetary experts" he was blaming those whom Keynes was to call the "classical economists" in 1936. Hence one cannot be sure which economists are charged with having adhered to principles "in conflict with the facts of everyday experience." How can we pinpoint passages which are thought to reflect the grave error that Johnson alleges? As Clower has pointed out, "Keynes . . . had to deal with doctrines of which no authoritative account had been given."* If it *is* mainly

* Johnson, relying on a recent article by Patinkin, seems to have the early Chicago school mainly in mind. (*See* p. 142).

a question of monetary economics, for instance, there were really considerable differences among such "classical" exponents as Mises, Marshall, Knight, Pigou, Viner, Roepke, Marget, Lavington, Ohlin, Palyi, Wicksteed, Angell, Hardy, Cannan, Eucken, Robbins, Kemmerer, Hayek, Simons, Hawtrey, Benjamin Anderson, Gregory, Benham, Browne (H. G.), and Mints.°

None of these was a minor figure. Of course, they may well have been all wrong or confused in some degree on one point or another. I have no doubts about that possibility. Monetary theory is by no means an easy subject. And they *were* necessarily ignorant of the jargon and models which have been developed by post-Keynesian economists! But it is by no means certain that the developments which have characterized economic theory since *The General Theory* have *really* contributed so very much to our understanding. As I see things, the truly vital issues are quite simple. In my judgment *the modern economists have, with laudable mathematical erudition, erected an imposing and analytically rigorous framework upon an inadequate foundation in respect of conceptual clarity.* At all events, I do not think that, using words in their everyday meaning, it can be shown that the economists I have listed above were more wrong than their contemporary critics on any important issue. Still less can I accept Clower's casual suggestion (quoted before) that the economics of these scholars was "a nearly decadent science." Moreover, I do not think that the policy implications of their analyses or their explicit recommendations can be shown to have been "demonstrably in conflict with the facts of every day experience," as Johnson charges. They were, I believe, all realistically and intelligently aware of the facts about which they speculated,° even though they may sometimes have seriously misunderstood them.

°I do not include here Cassel, Robertson, Henderson or Fisher because, although "classical" economists of stature, they tended to side with Keynes during the pre-*General Theory* period.

°On one important issue they were misled through official secrecy. (*See* pp. 141-3).

117

What they *can* be accused of (or praised for) is having assumed as almost unchallengeable that *it was beneficial for mankind to be served by an international monetary system based on contract, disciplined by social (i.e., market) pressures, and entrenched by powerful convention or law against currency debasement (inflation).* They may have given too high a priority to such objectives. But this must not be taken to imply that they were oblivious to the possibilities of the inflationary way out of depression. *They understood as clearly as their Keynesian critics did that inflation could mitigate or cure unemployment as long as costs lagged in relation to prices.* Hence the fact that they urged the avoidance of inflation like the plague (except for emergencies) does not mean that they failed to understand it.

Curiously, it was the Keynesians who seemed to deny, sometimes vehemently, that their proposals were inflationary. During the decade preceding *The General Theory,* Keynes' early disciples occasionally suggested "a little inflation." But with all the woolliness of *The General Theory* references to "true inflation," the Keynesians of the late thirties shunned any description of their recommendations as inflationary, in spite of the fact that they were disparaging non-inflationary policies and (in Harrod's phrase) removing "inhibitions against inflation."

In respect of economic policy in depression the basic controversy between the non-Keynesians and the Keynesian orthodoxy which supplanted it can be expressed as follows. The so-called "classical" orthodoxy of the 1920s and 1930s had two prongs to its depression policy implications: (1) to avoid the development of an inflationary situation which, requiring subsequent deflationary rectification *if contractual monetary obligations were to be honored,* would eventually precipitate depression through predictable resistances to the necessary price adjustments; and (2) if depression *had* emerged for this or other reasons, then in the light of insights derived from an understanding of Say's law, to encourage or

118

take steps to permit the pricing (of inputs and outputs) needed to restore the aggregate flow of *purchasing power* (as distinct from raising aggregate *"money-spending power"*—the money valuation of a given flow of purchasing power). The Keynesian orthodoxy on the other hand, instead of seeking recovery through policies calculated directly to restore aggregate purchasing power, aimed at reducing the measuring rod of value in which previous contracts had been concluded,* so that *an unchanged aggregate purchasing power would be expressed as a greater aggregate "money-spending power",** in the conviction that the increased spending would cause aggregate purchasing power to rise, even if less than proportionally to money-spending power.

To express the controversy in different terms, it can be said that *the "classical" theory of recession diagnosed what was wrong in a particular kind of human action, namely, in the pricing process. Monetary factors were regarded as vitally relevant, but always as subsidiary to a particular monetary phenomenon, namely, the pricing process—the valuing of services and goods in terms of money.* Problems such as recession or unemployment were to be blamed upon the existence of a framework of laws that permitted the determination of costs and prices in a socially deleterious manner, and the overriding of the collective interest by sectionalist interests. Fuller employment, they felt, had to be sought through fundamental reform of pricing or valuing activity. *Prosperity would not come about "automatically"* unless the institutional framework were deliberately planned with the aim

*As I have just asserted, they avoided putting it in this way. They stressed fiscal policy—*spending* (which they confused with *demanding*) which could be increased *via* budgetary deficits.

*Cannan's plea in 1924 for a distinction to be made between "purchasing power" and "money-spending power" did not, unfortunately, become part of the standard nomenclature of economics. Cannan pointed to the absurdity of saying that "the purchasing power of the German people was increased when they had trillions of marks to buy with."[2] As things are, modern economists still talk of "aggregate purchasing power" (or "aggregate demand") increasing through "newly activated money" or "newly created money."

119

of facilitating or permitting people to price their services, and those of their assets, in accordance with what they thought it profitable to offer one another, and to determine the composition and location of their assets, as well as their skills and domiciles, in the light of their interpretations of consumers' sovereignty. The Keynesians, on the other hand, avoided criticism of the framework and relied upon a sort of invisible hand which, they held, would be operative under "the maintenance of" (i.e., the inflationary dilution of) "aggregate demand" through fiscal and monetary policy and centralized "controls."

It is important to insist then that the economic theory which Keynes attacked did *not* teach or assume (as the present generation of economists seem mostly to have been taught) that "there was an automatic tendency towards full employment". H. G. Johnson states this explicitly. Possibly I am overlooking some passages in the works of the economists I named above (on p. 117), but my own search has failed to find any phrases which might be responsible for the misconception or justify the charge. For me, at any rate, the implication was *precisely the opposite,** namely, that unless government performed its classical role *there was an automatic tendency for groups acting in collusion to price their inputs or outputs in such a way that a cumulative tendency for economies to run down could be set in motion,* especially when the honoring of solemn promises to convert, following a "suspension" of currency convertibility, was accorded unquestioned priority.

Where pre-Keynesian teachings may have tended to mislead, was in the associated insight that *this automatic tendency towards recession* was aggravated by central banks giving way to political pressures for cheap money.

---

*That this *was* my own position prior to the appearance of Keynes' *General Theory* is proved by my *Economists and the Public*, 1936, and my claim in *The Theory of Idle Resources*, 1939, that it was "pure orthodoxy," a claim which was never challenged. *See* also, in particular, F. Benham, *British Monetary Policy* (1932).

As I have just explained, the "classical" economists thought that a period of inflationary ease engendered an inevitable retribution—deflationary rectification. But in spite of their awareness of man-made restraints on the co-ordinative valuing and pricing of inputs and outputs, they *did* believe (i) that it was *possible* to set values (and hence prices) of inputs and outputs under the disciplinary pressures of the market; (ii) that these pressures were conducive to the emergence of market-clearing prices and hence to full or optimal employment; and (iii) that economic policy *could* consciously aim at facilitating or encouraging the required pricing. *

It is on this pricing issue, however, that the theoretical cleavage between the "prevailing orthodoxy" and the Keynesians is most blatant. The latter thought that the inherent weaknesses of the system were to be found in freedom to value and price, not in private or collective restraints on that freedom*; although they held also, as I have already pointed out, that, if sufficient money-spending power were maintained through fiscal or monetary policy (i.e., if "effective demand" were adequate) the valuing and pricing system *would* function efficiently.

The "classical" objections to the Keynesian *policies* (which policies Johnson thinks *were* "sensible" for the 1930s), as distinct from Keynesian *economics*, were simply the time-honored objections to inflation. The real income transfers which inflation effected (a) from contractual claimants to residual claimants on the value of outputs, (b) from creditors to debtors, and (c) from those whose money incomes rose less than the

---

*The "classical" economists may in general have given insufficient weight to the political factor. But they certainly tried to interpret the concrete vote-acquisition phenomena of their day, even when they failed to perceive the policy consequences of a growing awareness of the profits to be won (by politicians and pressure groups) through realistic exploitation of universal suffrage. They never expected miracles.

*A difficulty is that at times Keynes and his disciples *were* assuming restraints on market freedom as causes of recession.

average to those whose incomes rose more than the
average, were regarded as *a crude and unjust* method
of enabling larger outputs to be priceable so as to cover
costs*; while the real income transfer effected (d)
from the ruled to the rulers was regarded as an un-
democratic method of taxation, with governments obtain-
ing funds thereby without overt parliamentary authoriza-
tion.

No economist questioned Keynes' assertion (announced
in *The General Theory* in challenging language as
though it was a revolutionary discovery*) that "labor"
tended to respond to money wage-rate offers rather
than to real wage-rate offers. Nor were any of his
critics skeptical about the corollary—that if at any
moment many real wage-rates were being held higher
than was consistent with the maintenance of the normal
wages and income flow, a reduction of real wage-rates
generally *via* inflation was a politically acceptable
(though crude and unjust) method of restoring that flow
(thereby restoring employment of men and assets). The
controversy was largely on the points: (a) how long the
money illusion would persist when the cost of living rose
discernibly; and (even more important) (b) *whether a
general system of economics could be usefully constructed on the assumption of a distress-precipitating
illusion* which, the non-Keynesians thought, wise policy
should have been planning to dispel. No one questioned
that the illusion was a crucial factor in the explanation
of depression and chronic unemployment. But a courageous
minority of economists did question the wisdom of *an
approach to economics in which resignation to or
acquiescence in an intolerable system of pricing labor in
a crucial segment of the economy was elevated into a
major premise.* To them it seemed preposterous to

* "Crude and unjust" partly because such a constraint of the wages and income flow is not due to *all* real wage-rates being too high but to *some*
being too high. Inflation hits the innocent as well as the culprits.

* Cannan referred to it, for instance, in 1933, in the passage quoted in Chap.
VIII, pp. 57-58.

accept that "just a little inflation" could restore prosperity while "just a little reasonableness in respect of wage-rates" had to be ruled out. I must stress that the recognition by such economists of the wages-restoring power of market-selected wage-rate adjustments did not mean that they were blind to the injustices caused thereby in many individual instances. It was a question of preferring temporary smaller injustices to greater permanent injustices.

Moreover, the pre-Keynesian economists feared the ultimate consequences of *"cheap money"* as *normal policy*; for that was what the Keynesians then seemed to be advocating. And they perceived that inflationary palliatives, *even if envisaged as temporary*, tended to create powerful vested interests in the continuance of inflation.* It was felt that future governments, anxious to escape from the sociological and political evils which inflation begets, would suddenly discover that they had (in Hayek's words) "a tiger by the tail." (*See* p. 113).

Certainly the pre-Keynesians were biased in favor of a rigid measuring rod of value. But just as a defined (i.e., rigid) ounce, pint or yard protected purchasers, so they thought that a money unit of defined value (such as the gold standard) could protect the public from discrimination, arbitrary dictates and totalitarian tendencies in government generally. They felt that, with all its shortcomings, the gold standard did provide a very effective safeguard against inflation, by reason of the power it conferred on every individual (or on every corporation under the "bullion" form of the standard) to

---

*Although, in spite of recognizing such dangers, they did not dogmatically rule out "temporary" inflation in all circumstances. Still less would they have ruled out "monetary flexibility" under my definition when, say, gold standard pressures were strongly deflationary, as they seem to have been in the United States between 1929 and 1933. Compare Cannan's reference (in 1932) to the world being "too stupid to prevent great declines in price levels" (quoted later in Chapter XVI, p. 128).

show lack of confidence in the official money unit by preferring gold to paper or deposits.

They recognized further that the gold standard had been remarkably effective in providing orderly and efficient (i.e., *cheap*) international economic relationships, with credit transactions and investment occurring on a global scale—an achievement for which the costly I.M.F. and the vast and incredibly expensive national bureaucracies which now monitor foreign exchange dealings have in fact turned out to be blatantly ineffective substitutes.

In 1936, I expressed the fear that Keynes of *The General Theory*, far from proving to be "an inspired missionary who is to rescue us from idolatry" could turn out to be "a false prophet who can lead us to damnation."[1] Nevertheless I do not think that any economist who shared such fears could predict, before the end of the Second World War, just how disastrously the actual adoption of Keynesian policies would drive us all along "the road to serfdom." It was only as concrete monetary experience of national currencies disciplined only by the I.M.F. agreements began to be judged that those economists who had resisted pressures to conform to the Keynesian creed began to see how justified their misgivings had been. They could then perceive that, relieved of any obligation to maintain a money unit of defined value, central banks were becoming political instruments manipulated for the profit of governments. The search for prosperity through collective control of "expenditure" accelerated a gradual destruction of the independence of central banks from the vote-acquisition process. (*See* below, pp. 141-142). The general fear then emerged that, once the inflation drug had been administered over any extended period, the economic system would become hopelessly addicted. Creeping, crawling, chronic inflation would seem to be essential for continuing economic health, and increasing doses would eventually appear necessary just to keep the system functioning. Ultimately, it was feared, a proliferation of totalitarian controls would become necessary to prevent individuals from using the remnants of the free market to protect themselves from some of the consequences. But for a long period the non-Keynesians seemed to be cowed by the sheer weight of academic opinion arrayed against them. *

If the Keynesian era is regarded as an experiment, then it can be claimed that the most pertinent difference between the "classical" and Keynesian remedies for depression is that *the "classical" ideas were never tried*—never submitted to experimental testing. * The blame for that may lie as much with the economists of the day as with the governments, a possibility which brings us back to my first interpretation of Johnson's diagnosis. The economists were so eager to be helpful and influential, and so anxious not to appear to be advising unsophisticated, unrealistic, "politically impossible" programs that they all made their own *tacit* allowances for the political factor. Unfortunately, their judgments about what would be politically acceptable differed so widely that they failed to speak with the united voice that normally characterizes, say, the expressed opinions of practitioners versed in medical science, and any authority with which they spoke was weakened. *

I do not think that any of the British economists who gave highest priority to the keeping of promises (i.e., the maintenance of convertibility) were surprised when the abandonment of that objective, followed by hesitant

---

*I confess that *I* was cowed. *See* the Preface to my *Keynesianism.*

*This was a principal theme of my *Economists and the Public* which appeared only a month or so after the publication of Keynes' *General Theory* in 1936.

*My recent book, *Politically Impossible. . . . . . ?*,[3] largely deals with this issue.

experiments in undisciplined monetary expansion, began to bring about a gradual recovery of outputs. The inflation set going through the era of competitive depreciation of national currencies in terms of gold (inaugurated by the British devaluation of September, 1931) raised prospective yields to investment in replacement and growth, which fear of strikes (or actual strikes) had for long been repressing. But in so doing it initiated the political tradition of validating duress-imposed costs by creeping inflation. Hence when British policy-makers in the 1930s are charged with lacking an adequate appreciation of the importance of money in facilitating economic growth, the word "money" is really a euphemism for "unanticipated inflation."

In addition to a general acceptance of the idea that there were great advantages, domestically and internationally, in the existence of a defined, contractually based measuring rod of value, the economists Keynes is supposed to have "debunked" recognized, tacitly or explicitly, the validity of Say's law. And it was against *this* aspect of the prevailing orthodoxy that Keynes' assault was really directed. Indeed, as I mentioned before, one of the most influential of the extremist Keynesians (Sweezy) admitted, in 1946, that the arguments of *The General Theory* would all be untenable if the validity of Say's law could be established.* If, then, Johnson's point is that it was acceptance of the "law of markets" which rendered "the prevailing orthodoxy" of the 1930s so futile, I must respectfully differ diametrically. I claim indeed to have shown that, *through an understanding of Say's law, an all-sufficient explanation of the source of depression and the way to avoid it is available.*

Admittedly, the economists whose insight into the working of that law toned their approach to the economic

---

*See p. 10.

126

problems of the 1930s could well have been gravely in error on some incidental yet practically decisive matters. Perhaps, then, it is in respect of subsidiary yet imperative issues that the economists Johnson disparages are thought of as unsatisfactory. To consider this possibility, I propose to examine the relevant teachings of a great scholar of the old school whom I have already quoted—Edwin Cannan.

1. R. Clower, *Monetary Theory*, p. 271.
2. E. Cannan, *Economic Journal*, March, 1924, p. 59n.
3. W. H. Hutt, *Politically Impossible . . . . . ?*, I.E.A., London, 1971.

XVI

SOME ASPECTS OF EDWIN CANNAN'S "ORTHODOXY"

Cannan's work (fallible though it is) is appropriate for my theme because it might be claimed for him that he was the staunchest of all among opponents of the inflationary solution for employment or recession. But did he for that reason try to explain "what were essentially monetary phenomena" by attributing the causes to "real phenomena"? Actually, it was because of the vagueness of the Keynesian monetary notions, as they were left after Keynes' *Treatise on Money*, that Cannan, in his Presidential Address to the Royal Economic Society in 1932, after disassociating himself from economists who believed "that great inconvenient changes of the price-level are as unavoidable as changes of weather," criticized "the reigning school of monetary experts." He charged that they had produced so much confusion that "the treasuries, which know very well, are afraid of medicine of which an overdose is easy."[1]

Cannan's suggestions about what had to be done (in his words) "if the world is too stupid to prevent great declines of price levels"[2] are not irrelevant to the reforms which are needed today.* In 1917, declaring that

*But the *present* world [this time, in *my* words] seems to be "too stupid to prevent" a creeping rise, or even an accelerating rise in the "price level."

128

he was "not a monetary expert" but maintaining that "it does not require a monetary expert to judge of the policy at present pursued . . . ," Cannan warned the British Board of Trade that, if inflation continued, and if the declared policy of restoring *effective* convertibility after the war were adhered to,* "complete collapse of prices and general gloom and depression are bound to come"[4] (after the war). But writing in February, 1920, before the postwar boom had broken, he argued that "if peoples' real wealth is decreasing I think it most important to diminish their money means at least equally, so as to make them appreciate their really unhappy position *and take the necessary steps to improve it,* instead of whining about profiteers"[5] [my italics]. It would be easy to ridicule such an attitude today but the words "at least equally" show that Cannan was not advocating deflation. He was here envisaging a measure of what I have termed "monetary flexibility." Modern critics of the pre-Keynesians ought to consider whether it could not be justly claimed that the eagerly accepted Keynesian *nostrum* enabled the world's rulers *to postpone taking what Cannan called "the necessary steps" for over four decades.* For the problems to which he was referring were just those for which I earnestly believe the coming generation will be forced somehow to find *non-inflationary* solutions.

Cannan's support for the return to an effective gold standard did not mean, then, that he was blind to the advantages of a more stable standard in a more civilized world. He warned (early in 1920) that "the thing most unlikely is that gold would be very stable. . . . If mankind want a stable standard," he wrote, "they must bestir themselves to make one."[6] The gold standard was, he

---

*About the time he was writing this, Cannan had been reprimanded by "a high authority" for "insinuating" that British currency notes were "inconvertible." He had actually asserted that they were "practically inconvertible" because it had been made a crime to export gold currency or melt it down for other purposes.[3]

wrote in 1923, certainly not "the most perfect standard which can and ever will, be devised by civilized man." One could claim for gold, he said, only a "very moderate amount of stability of value," and that had "been largely due to a fortunate collocation of circumstances, on the continuance of which it would be unsafe to rely."[7] He said many times (the first time, I think, in 1915), that he envisaged a more orderly future when the world would "eventually regulate its currency in some way instead of allowing it to be at the mercy of every gold discovery and every invention in the method of extracting it." (He wrote *this* in July, 1916).[8] The maintenance of a money unit of constant real value (which he sometimes termed the "general prices standard") was, he said, "naturally far more attractive . . . as an ideal to be worked for in the future."*[9] His hesitation about recommending immediate attempts to maintain the value of the money unit "stable in terms of commodities" (instead of stable in terms of gold) was that, before attempting to fashion such a system "we may as well make sure that we know how to do it." Also he was doubtful about the likelihood of other countries agreeing to any such standard. *[10] And although he agreed that "to tie the purchasing power of money to that of a single metal" was " . . . an expedient fit only for a barbarous age . . . ," can anyone "have any doubt," he asked, "that a barbarous age is precisely what we have at the moment to provide for? The cruder and simpler may serve us best for the present and immediate future. . . . For the advantage of exchange stability we ought to be prepared to sacrifice a good deal of the other stability—stability of domestic prices

*He did not regard such a monetary standard as "managed," except in the sense that the gold standard had to be managed.

*A few months later, Cannan wrote, "There is not the slightest chance of the various nations agreeing on any uniform system of limitation of currencies by prices which would give us the stability of international changes which we possessed before the war."[11]

between one time and another."[12] "Civilization cannot afford to do without a common standard of value. . . ." And when gold is later "superseded . . . by something more stable, its successor will be international also."[13] Nevertheless he believed (in 1925) that "the surrender of national autonomy in regard to price levels by the re-adoption of the gold standard" would "not in practice mean the abandonment of a fair prospect of stable levels, *but the restoration of a very effective barrier against gross inflation.*"[14] [My italics] He had little faith in governments not bound by some such standard. "Experience shows," he said, "that the general tendency to follow 'managed' currencies is towards rapid over-issue. . . . "[15] Three years before Cannan took this line Keynes himself had declared that he saw "no solution of (international) stabilization except this traditional solution—namely a gold standard in as many countries as possible."[16] But there had been no *doctrinaire dogmatism* on Cannan's part. "I do not say that gold must forever continue to be the best popular standard," he declared.[17] He simply thought (in 1920) that Britain had first to "get back to the gold basis and stand on it along with America," and only then "take part in the international consideration of means of stabilizing that basis itself."*[18] And in opposing the "just a little inflation" school, in February, 1924, and suggesting that "we should do well to go a *little* further" in keeping prices down,[20] he added that, if it would hasten the return to convertibility, "we should do well to submit to some devaluation"[21] (although those of us who knew him then were aware of his belief that the prestige of the City of London, which had been a factor of no small importance

---

*As early as 1915 he had forecast that "the remedy" for the obvious defects of gold "would have to be found in a cosmopolitan regulation of whatever may be adopted as the standard of value."[19]

to the British economy, would be adversely affected thereby*).

I ask now: In what senses can it be claimed that the implications of teachings such as Cannan's, which I have here sketched in his own words, were "not sensible," "demonstrably in conflict with the facts of everyday experience," or "clearly inconsistent with the most salient facts of reality," and so forth? Surely the answer is, only in the sense that governments and parliamentary oppositions were not *primarily* concerned with achieving "a plentiful subsistence for the people," or with prosperity, high wages and full employment, but with the retention or achievement of office, while it was becoming increasingly obvious that "a little inflation" (especially if it was not so described) could achieve contentment and electoral approval for an indefinite period ahead, without arousing angry reactions.

In my judgment at least, the politicians in the treasuries (and outside) were afraid, when Cannan was writing, of the vote-acquisition consequences of the sort of situation which reliance on Cannan-type teachings would create, while parliamentary oppositions were equally scared of solutions which would confront them with the hostility of powerful vested interests—especially the leaders of organized labor. And (as I have already stressed) the economists did not stand together.[22] Uncompromisingly "classical" notions were in fact inert.

*Cannan was not, of course, alone in this belief. It was widely held in influential circles. At times Keynes seemed to share the belief.

1. E. Cannan, "Not Enough Work for All," quoted from the reprint in Cannan, *Economic Scares*, London, P. S. King, 1933. pp. 40-41.
2. *Ibid.*, p. 41.
3. *An Economist's Protest*, London, P. S. King, 1927, pp. 114-116.
4. *Ibid.*, p. 109.
5. *Ibid.*, p. 220.

6. *Ibid.*, p. 229.
7. *Ibid.*, p. 355.
8. *Ibid.*, p. 96.
9. *Economic Journal*, June, 1924, p. 160.
10. *Ibid.*, March, 1924, p. 64.
11. *Ibid.*, June, 1924, p. 160.
12. *Ibid.*, pp. 160-161.
13. *An Economist's Protest*, p. 369.
14. *Ibid.*, p. 406.
15. *Ibid.*, pp. 406-7.
16. J. M. Keynes, in *Manchester Guardian Reconstruction Number*, April 20, 1922.
17. *Economic Journal*, June, 1924, p. 161.
18. *An Economist's Protest*, p. 218.
19. *Ibid.*, p. 17.
20. *Ibid.*, p. 368.
21. *Ibid.*, p. 369.
22. See Hutt, *Politically Impossible . . . ?*

XVII

THE BACKGROUND OF KEYNES' "GENERAL THEORY"

A critic of an earlier version of this essay has asked exactly what policies were implied by the non-Keynesian economics of the inter-war period in respect of the situation which prevailed in Britain in the 1920s and 1930s. I propose to answer in terms of the implications of Say's law; for tacit acceptance of that law is, as I have already said, what chiefly distinguished Keynesian and non-Keynesian thinking. We must remember that, on the whole, the non-Keynesians were content to provide the analysis and leave the formulation of policy to those who were expert in achieving electoral support. Had they been asked, however, "What do *you* suggest ought to be done to get us out of the present condition of chronic unemployment and stagnation?", they would have answered, I think, something like this:

> As far as the political situation permits, a basic re-reform of the pricing system needs to be undertaken, aimed specifically at releasing or creating incentives for the setting of market-clearing prices for all inputs

and all outputs. Our present unhappy condition is crying out for leadership—genuine leadership which does not shrink from the difficult task of explaining the initially unpopular changes required to achieve what Adam Smith called "a plentiful subsistence for the people."

But to appreciate the difficulties which would have confronted any statesman who had determined to grasp the nettle, let us look at the conditions which preceded the appearance of *The General Theory*.

There was no effective anti-monopoly law in Britain. Even the ancient common law against restraint of trade had been so emasculated by judicial decisions that it was of little consequence. But most serious of all in my judgment, duress-imposed labor costs in the unionized sector were gravely constraining profitable outputs in crucial industries, thereby repressing the wages and income flow, and forcing down market-clearing wage-rates in other fields. At the same time, the opinion-makers—press and politicians—were doing virtually nothing to encourage public sympathy for the required reforms. British industrial assets had not suffered serious *physical* damage during World War I, but their composition had been distorted to meet war demands; in many parts of the economy industrial plants were obsolescent; drastic modernization was often needed if British products were to compete as effectively in world markets as they had before 1914; yet the attitude of organized labor and the attitude of the politicians towards strike-threat exploitation were such as destroyed the prospect of "adequate" yields to the enormous capital investments which effective modernization demanded. Large-scale scrapping of existing plant would have been called for and its replacement with highly specific—i.e., non-versatile—plant; while the incentive to shoulder the formidable risk of supplying it was all too often eradicated through the fear of future strike-threat pressures. *

From time to time an editor, or some other public figure, would reprimand British industrialists for their lack of enterprise—their failure to electrify, or mechanize, or modernize. But I do not think that such admonishment ever referred, in that context, to the reality that, in the absence of radical reform, acceptable yields could hardly be predicted for capital devoted to expensive re-equipment. A situation had emerged in which entrepreneurs could expect that, *for the very reason that investment had been made in non-versatile assets, they could expect labor costs to be forced up sooner or later through the threat of a strike.*

This was the reason for the technological backwardness of British industry. The fact of (together with fear of) duress-determined labor costs, in crucial spheres, was repressing the means of recovery and rendering plausible government attempts to render high cost productive activities profitable by other means than the removal of privately imposed obstacles to lower costs.

Almost all the labor-economizing innovations which entrepreneurs did try to introduce in exploitable fields were bitterly fought by the unions. The union officials (as well as the rank and file) were oblivious to the reality that, ever since the invention of the wheel and the lever, the achievement of given outputs or objectives with fewer workers or a smaller value of capital assets had been multiplying the number of employment outlets at any given real-wage level.

But because influential leadership was lacking, the unionized sector was allowed to become riddled with

*The main theme of my recent book, *The Strike-Threat System* (Arlington House, 1973), is that *fear of strikes* does much more damage to the wages and income flow than *actual strikes or strike-threats* because that fear deflates prospective yields to the provision of the most effectively wage-multiplying types of assets, which tend to be the least versatile kinds.

demarcations, restraints on entry and restrictive practices generally. Moreover, official policy itself was indirectly fostering cost and price rigidities and, through the form taken by "unemployment compensation," creating wholly avoidable but apparently chronic unemployment.

The British labor market had indeed become chaotic. *Through the influence of the strike-threat in the "sheltered" industries* (i.e., in industries selling their outputs primarily at home, or for other reasons not subject to competition from abroad), *demands for the inputs and outputs of the "unsheltered" occupations were distressingly constrained.* But the blame for the consequential repressed wage-rate levels which could minimize the burden on workers employed in "unsheltered" activities, was typically attributed to the avarice of investors and not ascribed to the "sheltered" culprits. And when efforts were being made to mitigate the hardships of the most conspicuous among the "unsheltered" victims, namely, the unemployed coal miners, by trying to get the employed in that occupation to permit their idle comrades to price themselves into the labor market, Keynes, ignoring the humanitarian motives which had inspired the initiative, helped to sabotage it by crying that it violated "social justice"; and in this context he described the miners as victims of "the Economic Juggernaut." * He did not mean by "the Juggernaut," of course, the powerful unions which had been raising costs and prices in the sheltered sector.

His reckless injustice here illustrates what was really amiss—the deplorable situation which, according to Professor Johnson, classical teachings were power-

---

*Quoted in Melchior Palyi, *The Twilight of Gold.*[1] "The slogan 'social justice,'" wrote Palyi, has been used "for many purposes, legitimate or otherwise, but outside France scarcely, if ever, in favor of widows and orphans living on fixed pensions. Keynes never explained the meaning of this emotion-laden term."[2]

less to correct. I use the word "reckless" of Keynes' polemic because (in Melchior Palyi's phrase) "the men primarily responsible for sterling's return to the old parity were not 'reactionaries', insensitive to the sufferings of their fellow men. Nor did they consider unemployment as an 'incurable disease,' "[3] which is a libel that has been repeated more than once.

The "classical economists" of the 1930s, convinced though they were that chronic unemployment was avoidable (even under the deflationary pressures required for the return to gold and the maintenance of the reestablished parity), did not emulate Keynes' polemics. Perhaps they should have done so. They felt, I know, that it was hopeless to expect the politicians to heed them, unless they could concoct reasons for fashioning their recommendations in a politically acceptable form. But the politicians *knew* what the economists were thinking and teaching, namely, that labor's inputs were being priced inconsistently with full employment. The situation is made most abundantly clear in F. Benham's thoughtful but seldom quoted study, *British Monetary Policy*, published in 1932.[4]*

Because the pre-Keynesian economists diagnosed these *pricing phenomena* (presumably what Johnson means by "real phenomena") and abuse of unemployment compensation* as responsible for low employment stagnation, and because they had no faith in any Keynesian-type prescription, except as a temporary palliative, can we justly charge them with having been "hypnotized by the notion that money is merely a veil . . . "?

Let the reader consider the fact that the situation then ruling, when even Sidney and Beatrice Webb could

*In his very important recent book of the same title, *British Monetary Policy*, D. E. Moggridge does not refer to Benham's contribution, even in his his bibliography.

*See pp. 103-108.

privately describe the General Council of Trade Unions as "pigs,"[5] seems to be almost exactly duplicated in Britain today, in spite of about four decades of experiment with Keynesian policies. The main difference now is that recession has become compatible with inflation, so that monetary palliatives require an accelerating depreciation of the pound's purchasing power to achieve the vote-acquisition objective. The Chief Secretary to the Treasury (Mr. Patrick Jenkin) was arguing in late 1972 that, because inflation had been expected, its cessation would bring disastrous depression and unemployment. Hence, he claimed, a return to an incomes policy was inevitable. There was the same unwillingness to consider any policy of grasping the nettle and challenging the current acquiescence in strike-threat repression of the wages-flow together with inflationary validation of the consequences. I maintain that the pre-Keynesian economists whom Johnson appears to be disparaging were right in their conviction that attempts at inflationary rectification of a price-disco-ordinated economy would leave the crucial problem unsolved. Is not the present generation still confronted with that problem?

It is common for economists today to refer to the high costs required for adjustment to a convertible currency in 1925, and to blame for failing to predict the costs those economists who believed at that time that Britain should keep her promises and restore the prewar parity. But the formidable and costly difficulties actually experienced had, I believe, a political rather than an economic origin. The burden of transition did *not* arise out of the inevitable imperfections of the pricing system, but out of restraints upon it. The institutions of representative government under universal suffrage were undergoing revolutionary changes; the long view was being increasingly inhibited; and the chronic depression of the 1930s was one of the major consequences—a politically created pricing chaos which was experienced as the Great Depression.

D. E. Moggridge, in otherwise excellent studies of Britain's return to gold in 1925 and her attempts to persevere with the gold standard until September, 1931,[7] disparages the pre-Keynesian economists for their faulty judgment on the adjustment costs issue during the few years preceding 1925. But the real weakness of the economists of whom Moggridge is thinking must, I suggest, be attributed to their political assumptions, not their economic assumptions. In siding with the broad consensus that Britain could not think of "demeaning herself" (Cannan's words)* by breaking a solemn, long reiterated contract to aim at the restoration of the traditional parity with gold, they failed to foresee, or effectively to warn the community of the political implications—that is, of the extremes to which governments could be expected to go in order to avoid temporary unpopularity. Certainly the "classical economists" recognized and spoke out against the injustices to the unemployed and the repressed productivity caused by so-called "unemployment insurance." But they did not expressly warn of the likelihood that governments would tolerate private restraints or themselves impose restraints on the co-ordinative market pressures (including bank-rate pressures), pressures which could have restored prosperity (even if the gold parity accepted had meant that sterling was initially over-valued*). Of course, it was difficult for economists to predict how *future* governments would act. But following 1925, through passivity where action was called for, or through inter-

---

*I heard Cannan use these words (in 1921, I think) during a meeting of the "Sound Currency Association," at which he was a guest speaker, somewhere in the City of London. A few years later he would have reluctantly accepted a mild devaluation in return for an immediate return to convertibility. (*See* pp. 131-132).

*The belief that sterling *was* initially "over-valued" remains a matter of controversy.

vention where market freedom was called for, govern-ments were destined (after 1925) to magnify the burdens of change.

The faith of the non-Keynesians that, following the restoration of convertibility, unrestrained market pres-sures *could* create the required incentives for reduc-tions of such wage-rates and prices as might otherwise further depress the wages and income flows, has never been shown to be wrong. The reductions needed were far less drastic than those which had been brought about during 1920 to 1922 in order to restore some measure of pros-perity. Can the economists be blamed, then, for not stress-ing sufficiently forcibly the danger that *unrestrained* market pressures were destined to be suppressed? But what did happen was that private or sectional interests with vote-controlling power (acting through government or *via* monopolistic collusion and strike-threat duress) were allowed gravely to hinder the co-ordinative task of the pricing system. And can the orthodox economists be blamed, in particular, for failing to anticipate how, fol-lowing the adoption of convertibility, the tradition of dis-interested administration of the monetary and credit system would gradually become subject to Treasury pres-sures dictated by political expediency?

Even before the return to the gold standard, the Bank of England, until then a politically independent central bank, which had been performing, with judicial disin-terestedness and expert judgment, a vital yet purely technical task, was beginning to be subjected secretly to "moral suasion" by the Treasury and the Government.[*] The most important of the market pressures, the over-ruling of which multiplied the costs of adjustment to the re-established parity, were bank-rate pressures. But after 1925, "moral suasion" (unauthorized by any

[*]D. E. Moggridge's latest book, mentioned before, throws new light upon how the Bank of England was gradually coerced in spite of maintaining a posture of independence.[6]

legislation and termed "blackmail" by one commentator) impeded, with growing frequency, a crucial co-ordinative control. Again, I ask, who could have been expected to foresee this development?

A different form of disparagement of the non-Keynesian economists of the 1920s and 1930s refers to alleged defects of orthodox monetary theory. Economists like Patinkin, Johnson, and Clower make this charge.

It is true that there were economists of standing in Britain during the first decade of the inter-war period who believed that chronic unemployment may have been due in some measure to over-population, or who blamed it in part on the satiation of human wants, or who seemed to think that public works could serve as a remedy for depression. Johnson refers to them as evidence of the defects of pre-Keynesian economics. But the ideas mentioned here would, I think, have been rejected by all the economists I listed above (on p. 117), and certainly if they had really grasped the meaning of Say's law. When I think of the prevailing pre-Keynesian "orthodoxy," I envisage economists who, simply through familiarity with the economic literature of their day, understood Say's law (without necessarily having read Say or James Mill), who perceived the overriding importance and universal relevance of that law, and who tacitly tested every proposition of economics in the light of its implications.

The fact that there may have been substantial progress in monetary theory since the 1920s and 1930s does not mean that the "classical" teachings of that era had harmful implications. In fact, theoretical progress had been continuous since the beginning of the century. Cannan referred to it in 1924 when he described "the textbooks (on monetary theory) of years ago—not only elementary ones"—as "muddled, unsatisfactory. . . . " He stressed then "the improvement which has taken place," mentioning *inter alia* as important steps forward, recogni-

142

tion that "an expected change of prices causes prices to change" and recognition that the demand for money is a demand for holding it.[8] I am inclined to think that, had there been no Keynesian disturbance, even more progress in our understanding of monetary phenomena could well have been achieved. For subsequent monetary theorists seem to have felt constrained, even when they have thought of themselves as critics of Keynes, to use models, concepts and jargon derived from *The General Theory* and to try to reconcile their analyses with his.

Of course, not being prophets, economists in the 1920s and 1930s did not use the jargon and models of the dominant modern economics. In my judgment Patinkin's article, which Johnson thinks justifies his disparagement of the non-Keynesians (of the inter-war period and later), shows little more than that the early economists of the Chicago school did not use today's language.

But as I have already insisted, *the relevant content of the economics which Keynes attacked was not its monetary theory but its tacit acceptance of Say's law*; while if Johnson's reference to the failure of "the prevailing orthodoxy" envisages this tacit recognition of the relevance of Say's law, then his charge cannot be sustained. Looking back on the 1930s in Britain, and regarding the period as an historical economic phenomenon, I believe that, *whether or not contemporary non-Keynesians really perceived the full relevance of Say's law*, it offers a complete and wholly satisfactory insight into the nature of the chronic unemployment and the depression which emerged and persisted so disastrously. But if Johnson's contention can be interpreted (as I hope it can) to mean that the pre-Keynesian economists somehow failed *to explain what their economics explained*, I agree wholeheartedly.

A REHABILITATION OF SAY'S LAW

1. M. Palyi, *The Twilight of Gold*, Regnery, Chicago, 1972, p. 104.
2. *Ibid.*, pp. 104-6.
3. *Ibid.*, p. 104.
4. F. Benham, *British Monetary Policy*, P. S. King, London, 1932.
5. *Beatrice Webb's Diaries* (Ed., M. Cole), Longmans, 1956, Vol. II, pp. 283-4.
6. D. E. Moggridge, *British Monetary Policy*, C.U.P., 1972.
7. *Ibid.*, and *The Return to Gold, 1925*, C.U.P., 1969.
8. E. Cannan, *Economic Journal*, June 1924, pp. 156-7.

XVIII

CONCLUSION

It should now be clear that the initiating cause of emerging recession which Say's law explains is not the mere existence of widespread withheld productive capacity (wasteful idleness in assets and men or their wasteful use through confinement to "sub-optimal" activities). This is *in itself* the condition of chronic recession or depression. The relatively competitive sectors of the economy can adjust themselves to the wastefulness of defective pricing in other sectors without setting in motion further withholdings. But a wave of *new* withdrawals of inputs, each individual withdrawal tending to induce further withdrawals in other parts of the economy, in slowing down the rate of growth in input-flows, or causing an actual contraction in input-flows, must exercise a depressive influence upon the source of demands.

The path to recovery that is suggested by Say's law—institutional reforms to release, encourage or permit incentives for market-selected adjustments, (a) of "unduly" high wage-rates (which reduce the wages-flow and the average wage-rate), or (b) of other input prices which exceed market-clearing values, may appear to some as a cruel remedy. It is all too easy to *represent* it as such. But if "a little inflation" can rectify the situation, then "a little wage-rate reasonableness" can also rectify it. Those economists who have defended the inflationary maintenance or restoration of "aggregate effective demand" in order to combat the evil of "unemployment" have *never* advocated more than very mild inflation. They have always confidently expected a small depreciation of the real value of the money unit (and hence small reductions of real wage-rates) to be sufficient to restore "full employment" and the wages-flow. Hence they must recognize the corollary, namely, that the wage-rate cuts needed to raise or fully restore the average money wage-rate *without* inflation would also be small. * It is indeed an inescapable inference from the facts of inflation-induced recovery that in general elasticities of demands for labor must be high. If labor union officials as a body really wanted to avoid both cyclical layoffs and chronic unemployment, they would exercise leadership and habitually persuade the members of their unions not only to renounce the "wage-push" pressures which have for so long been repressing the wages-flow but, at appropriate times, to accept the temporary sacrifices needed to preserve or restore labor's earnings.

The condition under which an infectious withholding of productive services generates worsening idleness or idling of men or assets is basically a pricing phenomenon, not a monetary phenomenon. As long as the right to suppress the social discipline of market pressures by pricing inputs (including the inputs we call "marketing") in the private interest is tolerated (whether *via* government enactment; by strike, boycott or "predatory selling" duress; or by "peaceful" collusion), the automatic tendency to depression and unemployment which Say's law so clearly explains is inevitable. Powerful inducements to the *cumulative* withdrawal of purchasing power

---

*In some occupations large wage-cuts would be required to *maximize* (as distinct from to *restore*) the wages-flow.

(i.e., of "supplies") will persist irrespective of the rate at which an *anticipated* inflationary monetary policy may be causing money-spending power to increase. Keynes' legacy—the planned and progressive debasement of the money unit (of which we all feel so ashamed that we habitually resort to euphemistic descriptions of the process)—no longer effectively mitigates the depressive influence of input prices raised under the strike-threat or other forms of duress; for unions now make full allowance for the inflation that their pressures make expedient.

Incomes policies offer no solution. The whole history of attempts in that direction in Britain, the United States and elsewhere demonstrates their futility. For just as the poverty-creating consequences of the strike-threat system are tolerated ultimately because of the enormous vote-control power of those who administer that system, so must the political determination of wage-rates and prices be enforced for the private benefit of union leaders. And it is these organizations which must accept chief blame for the expediency of the chronic currency debasements that are sapping the economic health of the western communities. *

There can be no solution until opinion-makers recognize that recovery from recession can be achieved only if all employment outlets, however lowly paid initially, can be peacefully filled. And the wage-rate and price adjustments then needed will have to be market-selected, protected from strike-threat or other duress, and not imposed through such crude initiatives as Cost of Living Councils, Price Commissions and Pay Boards.

I have tried to show that Say's law explains the fundamental reality on which an economic science relevant to an advanced division of labor has to be erected. An under-

*See W. H. Hutt, *The Strike-Threat System*, Chapter 17.

standing of its implications by the world's opinion-makers could result in an unparalleled amelioration of the material well-being and economic security of mankind. More important, it could bring within reach an unprecedented improvement in the quality of life. For the attainment of those non-material ends which non-economists tend to call "non-economic" is facilitated, not frustrated, by advances in the physical welfare of the people.

Index

Allen, W. R., 11n, 29n.
Anderson, B. M., 24, 117.
Angell, J. W., 117.

Benham, F. C., 117, 120n, 138, 144n.
Blaug, M., 2, 3n, 11n.
Bodkin, R. G., 104.
Browne, H. G., 84, 84n, 117.

Cannan, E., 57-59, 60n, 61n, 78, 85, 96,
    116-117, 119, 122n, 123n, 127, 127n,
    Chapter XVI, 140, 140n, 142, 144n.
Cassel, G., 117n.
Clower, R. W., vi, 9, 9n, 12n, 48-50,
    52n, 57-58, 61, 66, 73n, 74n, 78, 81n,
    82, 85-86, 88n, 95, 100, 102-103,
    116-117, 127, 142.

Eucken, W., 117.

Fisher, I., 117n.

Gregory, T., 117.
Grossman, H. I., 104, 107, 109n.

Haberler, G., 9.
Hardy, C. O., 117.
Hawtrey, R. G., 117.
Hayek, F. A. von, 113n, 117, 123.
Henderson, H. D., 81n, 117n.
Hume, D., 4, 7n.

Johnson, H. G., 1, 2, 9, Chapter XIV,
    116, 120-121, 126, 137, 139, 142-143.

Kemmerer, E. W., 117.
Keynes, J. M., vi, 1-3, 6-11, 18-19,
    24-26, 38, 42n, 48, 50, 53-57, 63-66,
    70, 72, 83, 85, 103-104, 107-128, 131,
    132n, 134, 137-138, 143, 147.
Knight, F. H., 117.
Korner, E., 24
Kuh, E., 104.

Lange, O., 34.
Lavington, F., 84, 84n, 88n, 117.
Leijonhufvud, A., vi, 3n, 9, 11n, 19n,
    48, 48n, 54-61, 66-78, 82-83, 89-103.

Marget, A., 117.
Marshall, A., 117.
McCord Wright, D., 9.
McCulloch, J. R., v, 4n.
Mercier de la Rivière, 6.
Mill, James, 3n, 4, 4n, 7n, 11n, 25, 29n,
    142.
Mill, J. S., 3, 4n, 24, 26, 32.
Mints, L. W., 117.
Mises, L. von, 117.
Moggridge, D. E., 138, 140-141, 144n.

Neisser, H., 31, 34, 42n.

Ohlin, B., 117.

Palyi, M., 117, 137n, 138, 144n.
Patinkin, D., 24n, 48n, 57, 83, 111, 116n,
    142, 143.
Pigou, A. C., 2, 117.

INDEX

Quesnay, F., 34n, 42n.

Ricardo, D., 4n.
Rivière, Mercier de la, 6.
Robbins, L., 117.
Robertson, D. H., 117n.
Robinson, Joan, 55n.
Roepke, W., 117.

Schumpeter, J. A., 3n, 4-5, 11n.
Senior, W. N., 4n.
Shenoy, Sudha, 113n.
Simons, H. C., 117.
Smith, Adam, 2, 4, 7n, 46, 135.
Sowell, T., v, 3n, 11n, 35-36, 42n.
Spengler, J. J., 6, 11n, 29n.
Sweezy, P., 10, 12n, 126.

Thornton, H., 4.
Tucker, J., 6.
Turgot, A. R. J., 7.

Viner, J., 117.

Walras, L., 10, 15, 33, 34n, 46-47, 51-52, 67n, 89-91, 95-96.
Webb, S. and B., 138-139.
Wicksell, K., 22n.
Wicksteed, P., 117.
Wright, D. McCord, 9.

Yeager, Leland, 9, 48n, Chapter IX, 66, 73n, 77n, 83, 88n, 106, 109n.

150